KINGSTON REGISTER

Gloucester and
Mathews Counties, Virginia,
1749-1827

Compiled by
EMMA R. MATHENY
and
HELEN K. YATES

CLEARFIELD

Reprinted for
Clearfield Company, Inc. by
Genealogical Publishing Co., Inc.
Baltimore, Maryland
1991, 1996, 2004

Originally Published: Richmond, Virginia, 1963
© 1963 Emma R. Matheny and Helen K. Yates
All Rights Reserved
Reprinted, with permission, by the
Genealogical Publishing Co., Inc.
Baltimore, 1979
Reprinted from a volume in The Public Library
of Fort Wayne and Allen County, Indiana
Library of Congress Catalogue Card Number 78-71106
International Standard Book Number 0-8063-0832-X
Made in the United States of America

Dedicated to

John C. Matheny

and

S. Wirt Yates

for their patience and understanding of our neglect while this book was being compiled.

PREFACE

In the development of colonial Gloucester County, Virginia, and its parishes, there is a complete absence of the successive subdivision and combination of territory that mark the history of the parent county, York, and its parishes. Not only did Gloucester County maintain its original area throughout colonial times, but it also maintained its primary subdivision into four parishes. These four parishes, Petsworth, Abingdon, Ware, and Kingston, appear to have been simultaneously created shortly after the county's formation, and retained their original boundaries unchanged up to the close of the colonial era.

Petsworth was the most westerly of these four parishes, while Ware lay just north of Abingdon in the middle of the county and Kingston occupied the entire section east of North River. In 1791, after the Colonial period, Kingston Parish was cut off to form the present county of Mathews. (Colonial Churches of Tidewater Virginia by George Carrington Mason.)

The first recorded mention of the county by name seems to be in a land grant in the Virginia Land Office records, dated 21 May 1651, and this year is generally accepted as the date of the county's formation. No act of assembly specifically establishing any of the four parishes in Gloucester has come to light, but it is probable that they were simultaneously created by county court order in accordance with Act IX of the Grand Assembly of March 6, 1655/6, which required that, "all counties not yet laid out into parishes shall be divided into parishes the next county court." (Hening, Statutes at Large, Vol. 1, p. 400.)

The first order in the Kingston Parish Vestry Book, dated 15th November 1679, reveals the existence of a church building the location of which is mentioned in a renewal patent of the 5th September in the above year. Called the North River Chapel, it apparently stood on the site of a later church of the same name located two miles south of the highway bridge over North End Creek, one of the headwaters of North River. The neck of land between North River and Blackwater Creek is still called Chapel Neck.

Toward the close of the earlier part of the Kingston Parish Vestry Book is found the first indication that the parish had more than one church building, in the record of, "a vestry held the 29th of September 1715 at the Eastermost River Church." Further entries refer to these two churches as the New Church and Old Church, or the Upper Church and Lower Church. The present Trinity Church and Christ Church, modern Episcopal structures in Kingston Parish, both stand upon the sites of colonial houses of worship which must have been the two churches mentioned in the vestry book.

From 1677 to 1691 the Rev. Michael Typerios and James Bowker were ministers, but when their ministries began or ended is not known. In the year 1740 the Rev. John Blacknal appears on the first page of an imperfect vestry book. It cannot be ascertained how much of the vestry book was lost, or how long Mr. Blacknal may have served before 1740. He died in 1747, and was succeeded in 1750 by the Rev. John Dixon, the Rev. Richard Locke having served meanwhile for three months. In the year 1770 Mr. Dixon resigned and died in 1777. Four applicants appeared for the parish, the Revs. Thomas Baker, Thomas Field, Arthur Hamilton, and Archibald Avens, of whom Mr. Field was chosen, Mr. Baker having previously served three months. In the year 1778 Mr. Field either died or resigned, and the Revs. Robert Read and William Dunlop were candidates - the former being chosen. In the year 1784 the Rev. Thomas Hopkinson became the minister, and in the year 1789 the Rev. James McBride. In 1794 the Rev. Armistead Smith became the minister and was ordained by Bishop Madison. (Vestry Book of Kingston Parish.)

The parish vestry in colonial Virginia was aristocratic in character, being composed of the wealthiest and most prominent men in the parish. From the year 1677, vestrymen serving Kingston Parish as recorded in the vestry book were: Richard Dudley, James Ransone, James Hill, Sands Knowles, George Burge, Thomas Bayley, Robert Elliot, Ambrose Dudley, Peter Ransom, John Billops, William Tompkins, Charles Jones, John Coot, Humphrey Tompkins, Edmund Roberts, George Dudley, John Hayes, Hugh Gwinne, Robert Barnard, Charles Debrum, William Marlow, Humphrey Joye Tabb, William Armistead, Kemp Plumer, Gwinne Reade, Thomas Hayes, William Tabb, Charles Blacknal, John Peyton, Captain Thomas Smith, Kemp Whiting, George Dudley, John Armistead, James Ransom, Robert Tabb, William Plummer, William Armistead, Edward Hughes, Francis Armistead, John Willis, Gabriel Hughes, John Billip, Walter Keeble, Edmund Custis, Edward Tabb, John Dixon, Thomas Peyton, Robert Mathews, Dudley Cary, Mordecai Throckmorton, James Booker, Josiah Dean, Thomas Smith, Jr., Samuel Williams, Joel Foster, Armistead Smith, Robert Cary, Thomas Tabb, Richard Gregory, James Bibber, Sands Smith, John Cary, Wilton Glasscock.

Gloucester County possesses few colonial county records, nearly all its archives having been destroyed by fire, either in 1820, through the burning of the county clerk's office, or in 1865, at the fall of Richmond, where they had been sent for safe-keeping. The register of Kingston Parish is one of the few extant colonial church records. Dating from 1749, the last entry was made in 1827. A photostat copy of the original Kingston Parish Register is maintained in the archives of the Virginia State Library, and it is from the photocopy of this ancient record that the compilers have painstakingly copied the births, deaths, and marriages recorded therein.

Joyce H. Lindsay

Richmond, Virginia
April 15, 1963

INTRODUCTION

The Kingston Parish Register shows the ravages of time, but the fact that it is still in existence and has been preserved through the years is just short of a miracle. Gloucester, founded in 1651, and Mathews, cut off from Gloucester in 1791, have so little left of the early records that Kingston Parish Register is of real importance.

The first four pages are in very bad condition, torn in places and illegible in others. These pages are marked A, B, C, and D. There are a few pages missing: pages 91-102, 111-150 and 181-216 are no longer in the book. The spelling is irregular. The compilers have copied the spelling just as it is shown in the Register and the reader would do well to check all spelling of the surnames. At times the compilers felt the urge to correct the spelling; but if this was to be "THE Kingston Parish Register", it had to be copied the way the name appeared in the original record and not the way they felt it should be. Some of the apparent errors are underlined.

There is one important item the compilers would like to call to the attention of the reader: The right to perform marriage ceremonies was the exclusive prerogative of the parish ministers. It was generally admitted that no valid marriage ceremony could be performed except by the clergymen of the Established Church. Therefore, the marriages and births outside the Episcopal church was frowned upon and not recognized. In some cases, the parish minister would record the births of children from such "outside" marriages as illigitimate, depending upon how strongly he felt about the matter. In this book the births of illegitimate children are recorded just as they appear in the original register, but the reader is urged to keep in mind the above statement.

Mrs. Matheny and Mrs. Yates have copied about 530 marriages, 1750 births and 120 deaths - a record worth preserving, especially from an area where research is difficult.

The compilers wish to acknowledge their appreciation to Mrs. Joyce H. Lindsay without whose inspiration this work would not have been completed; and to the Staff of the Virginia State Library for their help and cooperation.

MARRIAGES

Adams, James and Mary Window, Feb. 13, 1777. Banns. p. 234

Adams, Zechariah and Ann Ripley, Sept. 26, 1771. Banns. Thomas Feilde, Rector. p. 228

Alleman, John and Milly_____, Dec. 9, 1763. p. 224

Amys, William and Ann Hill, Oct. 16, 1761. p. 223

Anderson, Edward and Frances Marchant, Feb. 16, 1750. Banns. By Rev. Richard Locke. p. 217

Anderson, Edward and Susanna Davis, May 4, 1777. Banns. p. 234

Anderson, John and Lucretia Dickson, May 17, 1777. Banns. p. 234

Anderton, Mark and Mary Treacle, Oct. 25, 1761. p. 223

Anderton, William and Jenny Hall, July 8, 1764. p. 225

Anderton, William and Mary Hunley, Dec. 25, 1776. Banns. p. 234

Angel, Benoni and Frances Holder, May 2, 1777. Banns. p. 234

Armistead, Currel and Margaret Michen, Dec. 29, 1770. Banns. In Kingston Parish, Gloucester Co. by Rev. Thomas Baker

Armistead, Francis and Dorothy Reade, Feb. 2, 1766. p. 225

Armistead, George and Lucy Palmer (widow), Dec. 12, 1770. License. In Kingston Parish, Gloucester Co., by Rev. Thomas Baker. p. 228

Armistead, Harkey and Miss Mary Tabb, June 19, 1773. License. p. 230

Armistead, John and A____ _____, June 29, 1762. p. 223

Armistead, Richard and Elizabeth Jervis, Feb. 11, 1770. p. 227

Armistead, _____ and _____, Oct. 12, 1753. p. 219

Ashbury, Joseph and Letitia Hodges, Nov. 16, 1752. License. p. 219

Ashbury, Joseph and Mary Basset, Mar. 12, 1776. Banns. p. 233

Atherton, Charles and Elizabeth Perrott, Feb. 12, 1774. Banns. p. 231

Ayres, John and Johanna Harris, Mar. 9, 1776. Banns. p. 233

B

Bagwell, Samuel and Dorothy Machen, Dec. 19, 1762. License. p. 224

Baillie, Robert and Elizabeth Angel, Nov. 6, 1773. Banns. p. 230

Baley, Matthew and Elizabeth Williams, Feb. 15, 1774. Banns. p. 231

Banks, John and Elizabeth Steward, Aug. 28, 1763. p. 224

Barton, John and Hester Bohannon, Sept. 18, 1750. Banns. By Rev. Richard Lock. p. 217

Basset, William and Mary Minter, Feb. 19, 1773. Banns. p. 230

Baster, John and Elizabeth Pew, Feb. 23, 1755. p. 220

Beard, John and Dorothy Hudgin, Dec. 25, 1766. p. 226

Bell, Peter and Mary Longest, Dec. 7, 1754. p. 220

Bell, Peter and Elizabeth Longest, Aug. 8, 1772. Banns. p. 229

Bernard, Peter and Frances Dudley, Aug. 22, 1758. License. p. 222

Bernard, Robert and Rose Pilot, Apr. 2, 1753. License. p. 219

Billups, Humpry and Frances Blacknall, Dec. 19, 1760. License. p. 223

Billups, John and Mary Lilley, Mar. 31, 1757. p. 221

Billups, John and Elizabeth Beverley Whiting, Apr. 11, 1776. Banns. p.233

Billups, Robert and Ann Ransone, May 7, 1755. License. p. 220

Billups, Robert and Elizabeth Eddens, Nov. 21, 1758. p. 222

Billups, Robert and Mrs. Sarah Gibson (widow), July 28, 1770. License. In Kingston Parish, Gloucester Co. by Rev. Thomas Baker. p. 228

Billups, Thomas and Mildred Lilly, June 16, 1769. p. 227

Blake, James and Ann Hudgen, Sept. 21, 1771. Banns. By Thomas Feilde, Rector. p. 228

Blake, Jonathan and Elizabeth Lewis, Sept. 27, 1768. p. 227

Blake, William and Dorothy Flippin, June 3, 1761. p. 223

Blake, William and Elizabeth Mullins, May 20, 1775. Banns. p. 232

Blunt, Bartholomew of Ware Parish and Elizabeth Hunley of this Parish, July 2, 1776. Banns. p. 233

Bohannan, William and Mary Gordon, May 9, 1761. p. 223

Boram, Edward and Frances Machen, Jan. 22, 1767. p. 226

Boram, John and Johanna Thomas, May 15, 1775. Banns. p. 232

Boss, Joseph and Sarah Shipley, Feb. 4, 1775. Banns. p. 232

Boswell, Panranparabo and Sarah Going, Feb. 1, 1756. p. 220

Boswell, Robert and Sukey Davis, Mar. 13, 1763. p. 224

Bramham, Richard and Sarah Mason, May 21, 1769. p. 227

Bridge, John and Ann Beard, Mar. 8, 1756. p. 221

Bridge, Joshuah and Rebecca Miller, Apr. 4, 1765. p. 225

Bridge, William and Ann Machen, Oct. 30, 1777. Banns. p. 234

Bridges, Richard and Susannah Bridges, Dec. 23, 1769. p. 227

Bristo, Henry and Elizabeth Willis, Oct. 18, 1756. p. 221

Bromley, Augustin and Mary Hudgin, Nov. 20, 1766. p. 226

Bromley, Robert and Sarah Williams, Nov. 1, 1772. Banns. p. 229

Brommel, Peter and Elizabeth Hudgin, Nov. 11, 1762. p. 224

Brooks, George and Susannah Davis, May 18, 1756. p. 221

Brooks, Joseph and Frances Murry Killigrew, Dec. 29, 1754. p. 220

Brooks, Thomas and Mrs. Mary Blacknall, Dec. 16, 1749, by Rev. Richard Locke. License. p. 217

Brounley, Archibald and Frankey Keyes, Sept. 20, 1769. p. 227

Brounley, Archibald and Sarah Keys, Jan. 16, 1772. Banns. p. 229

Brounley, James and Elizabeth Jarvis, Sept. 4, 1768. p. 227

Brounley, James and Sarah Brounley, Dec. 31, 1775. Banns. p. 232

Brounley, Thomas and Abigail Soaper, Apr. 3, 1774. Banns. p. 231

Brounley, William and Elizabeth Minter, Dec. 23, 1771, by Thomas Feilde, Rector. Banns. p. 229

Brounly, Archibald and Sarah Hudgin, Nov. 19, 1764. p. 225

Brown, Christopher and Lucy Macken, Jan. 19, 1771 by Thomas Feilde, Rector. License. p. 228

Brown, Francis and Susanah Iveson, March 31, 1766. No. Lic. to be had 20/ p. 226

Brown, Francis (widower) and Betty Jordan Foster (widow), Feb. 9, 1777. Banns. p. 234

Brown, George and Dorothy Gayle, July __, 1772. Banns. p. 229

Brown, Robert and Ann Gayle, July ___, 1772. Banns. p. 229

Brown, William and Judith Longest, Sept. 30, 1762. p. 224

Brown, William and Mary Masters, Mar. 8, 1763. p. 224

Brownly, William and Betty Soaper, Feb. 21, 1755. p. 220

Brumley, Edward and Elizabeth Hudgin, Jan. 20, 1761. p. 223

Brumley, William and Sarah Bromley, Feb. 3, 1761. p. 223

Buckner, Mordicia and Mrs. Mary Tabb, Jan. 10, 1765. License. p. 225

Buckner, Thomas William and Elizabeth Smith, Sept. 11, 1773. Banns. p.230

Burge, William and Joyce Banks, Sept. 24, 1776. Banns. p. 233

Burgess, John and Mary Davis, June 12, 1764. p. 225

Burton, Charles and Ann Billups, July 18, 1776. Banns. p. 233

Bush, George and Mary Mullins, Apr. 2, 1774. Banns. p. 231

Bush, Richard and Sarah Summers, May 6, 1759. p. 222

C

Callis, Ambrose and Mary Miller, Oct. 30, 1768. p. 227

Callis, Richard and Joyce White, May 31, 1775. Banns. p. 232

Callys, Jos___ and Elizabeth Hurst, Oct.___, 1750, by Rev. Richard Locke, Banns. p. 217

Camp, Thomas and Mary Tomkins, Sept. 16, 1755. License. p. 220

Carey, John and Dorothy Dudley, Apr. 23, 1755. License. p. 220

Carney, William and Ann Morgan, June 28, 1772. Banns. p. 229

Carter, George and Jane Elliot, June 7, 1755. License. p. 220

Carter, James and Dorothy Elliot, Feb. 15, 1777. Banns. p. 234

Cary, Dudley and Lucy Tabb, Nov. 11, 1775. Banns. p. 232

Chapman, Henry and Mildred Pallister, Dec. 15, 1760. p. 223

Chase, John and Elizabeth Thomas, Sept. 12, 1776. Banns. p. 233

Clark, Richard and Elizabeth Bohannon, Feb. 17, 1755. p. 220

Collins, John and Mary Jervis, Dec. 31, 1772. Banns. p. 229

Colvin, William and Hannah Fordam, Oct. 18, 1769. p. 227

Cook, Mordicai and Mary Hayes, Oct. 7, 1755. License. p. 220

Cooke, Ignatius and Averilla Hudgen, Oct. 31, 1769. p. 227

Cosby, James (of Ware Parish) and Jane Dudley, Feb. 20, 1752. p. 219

Cowper, Abraham and Mary Cuningham, May 26, 1759. License. p. 222

Coye, Charles M. and Jo_____ _____, May 26, 1762. p. 223

Crawley, Abraham and Dorothy Putman, Apr. 23, 1753. p. 219

Cray, Richard and Ann Hudgins, May 17, 1770, in Kingston Parish, Gloucester County by Rev. Thomas Baker. Banns. p. 228

Cray, John and Sarah Hunley, May 16, 1774. Banns. p. 231

Culley, Ralph and Mary Singleton, Nov. 6, 1776. Banns. p. 233

Culley, _____ and Mary Armistead, Feb. 5, 1776. p. 225

Curtis, Christopher and Anna Dudley, Aug. __, 1753. License. p. 219

Curtis, Christopher and Johannah Plummer, Sept. 28, 1756. License. p. 221

D

Dale, John and Judith Jarvis, Feb. 3, 1775. Banns. p. 232

Darricot, William of Hanover and Catherine Finch of Petsworth, _____1768. License. p. 226

Davis, Edward and Sarah Davis, Dec. 14, 1762. License. p. 224

Davis, Edward and Frances Davis, Dec. 10, 1765. p. 225

Davis, Humphry and Martha Christian, Jan. 5, 1768. p. 226

Davis, Isaac and Anne Gayle, Feb. 27, 1750, by Rev. Richard Locke. Banns. p. 217

Davis, Isaac and Rebecca Armistead, Jan. 9, 1772. Banns. p. 229

Davis, Isaac and Mrs. Rose Hunley (widow), Dec. 19, 1773. License. p. 230

Davis, James and Ann Davis, June 15, 1771 by Thomas Feilde, Rector. Banns. p. 228

Davis, John and Elizabeth Davis, June 22, 1755. p. 220

Davis, Joseph and Ann Willis, May 9, 1767. p. 226

Davis, Thomas and Lucretia Lewis, Aug. 17, 1769. p. 227

Davis, _____ard and Sarah White, Apr. 10, 1757. p. 221

Dawson, Christopher and Ann Brooks, June 25, 1758. p. 222

Dawson, James and Mary Hudgin, Mar. 26, 1769. p. 227

Dawson, John and Hester Merchant, Dec. 22, 1760. p. 223

Deal, James of Abingdon and Mary Pursley of this Parish, Aug. 17, 1774. Banns. p. 231

Deane, Josiah of the Co. of Norfolk and Rosanna Lilly of this Parish, Feb. 26, 1774. License. p. 231

Deforrest, Cornelius and Elizabeth Skelton, Oct. 16, 1751. License. p. 218

Degge, John and Joyce Davis, Mar. 23, 1775. Banns. p. 232

Degge, John and Ann Miller, Apr. 7, 1776. Banns. p. 233

Degge, Joshuah and Elizabeth Degge, Oct. 13, 1762. p. 224

Degge, William and Mary Gayle, June 23, 1768. p. 227

Delaney, Edward and Mildred Banks, Nov. 1, 1776. Banns. p. 233

Dixon, John and Miss Elizabeth Peyton, Feb. 6, 1773. License. p. 230

Dixon, (Capt.) Thomas and Miss Sarah Hankins, Dec. 8, 1774. License. p.231

Dixon, William and Elizabeth Merchant, Oct. 27, 1774. Banns. p. 231

Dobson, Robert and Bathsheba Weston, May 25, 1777. Banns. p. 234

Dowdy, Lawrence and Elizabeth Hudgin, May 19, 1766. p. 226

Dudley, George and Dorothy Tabb, Sept. 7, 1758. License. p. 222

Dudley, George Alexander and Mary Billups, June 11, 1766. No. Lic.26/ p. 226

Dudley, John and Elizabeth Lucas, May 16, 1752. p. 219

Dudley, Thomas and Sarah Dudley, Jan. 1, 1766. p. 225

Dudley, Thomas of the Co. of King & Queen and Mrs. Mary Curtis of this Parish, May 13, 1775. License. p. 232

Dudley, William and Sally Hill, Mar. 5, 1761. p. 223

Dudley, William and Sally Jarvis, Sept. 15, 1771 by Thomas Feilde, Rector. Banns. p. 228

Dudley, William Todd and (Miss) Mary Muscow Jones, June 10, 1775. License. p. 232

Dunla_____, William and _____, Dec. 25, 1763. p. 224

DuPlese, Charles and Amy Rice, Apr. 13, 1770, in Kingston Parish, Gloucester Co. by Rev. Thomas Baker. Banns. p. 228

Dye, Richard and Sukey Putman, Dec. 25, 1762. p. 224

E

Eddens, Dawson and Letitia Billups, Jan.___ 1768. p. 226

Eddens, John and Elizabeth Billups, Aug. 6, 1760. p. 223

Eddens, Samuel and Nancy Callis, Oct. 20, 1770, in Kingston Parish, Gloucester Co. by Rev. Thomas Baker. Banns. p. 228

Edmundson, Robert of Essex Co. and Miss Anna Elliot of Kingston Parish, June 9, 1750 by Rev. Richard Locke. License. p. 217

Edwards, Charles and Elizabeth Morgan, Dec. 3, 1771 by Thomas Feilde, Rector. Banns. p. 229

Edwards, Thomas Whiting and Mary Perrot, Dec. 25, 1776. Banns. p. 234

Elliot, William and Judith Dudley, May 22, 1766. No License on account of Stamp 20/   p. 226

Elliott, William and Miss Mary Cary, May 13, 1773. License. p. 230

Enos, Francis and Mrs. Sarah Baker (widow), Jan. 26, 1774. License. p.231

Evans, John and Winifred Longest, Feb. 3, 1771 by Thomas Feilde, Rector. p. 228

Evans, John and Judith Cleaver, Aug. 23, 1772. Banns. p. 229

Evans, Lewis and Judith Lucas, July __, 1772. Banns. p. 229

Evans, William and Anna Brown, Dec. 15, 1770, in Kingston Parish, Gloucester County by Rev. Thomas Baker. Banns. p. 228

F

Fercharson, Philip and Jane Iveson, Oct. 22, 1761. License. p. 223

Filyoung, George and Elizabeth Degge, Oct. 3, 1753. p. 219

Fitchet, Daniel of Northampton and Sarah Marchant, Dec. 8, 1749, by Rev. Richard Locke. p. 217

Fitchet, Thomas and Ann Chamberlain, Jan. 28, 1774. Banns. p. 231

Fitzhugh, George and Frances Tabb, Nov. 25, 1775. Banns. p. 232

Fletcher, John and Mary White, Dec. 17, 1769. p. 227

Fletcher, Thomas and Ann White, Apr. 14, 1753. p. 219

Flippin, Humphry and Sarah Davis, Nov. 18, 1766. p. 226

Flippin, Humphry and Mary Keys, Sept. 24, 1775. Banns. p. 232

Flippin, Thomas and Dorothy Brookes, Feb. 23, 1769. License. p. 227

Forrest, Abraham and Mary Forrest, Feb. 27, 1750, by Rev. Richard Locke. Banns. p. 217

Forrest, Abraham and Sarah Longest, Dec. 1, 1772. Banns. p. 229

Forrest, Edmond and Mary Weston, July 25, 1776. Banns. p. 233

Forrest, George and Mary Hunley, Aug. 16, 1770, in Kingston Parish, Gloucester Co. by Rev. Thomas Baker. Banns. p. 228

Forrest, Henry and Anna Billups, Dec. 21, 1771 by Thomas Feilde, Rector. Banns. p. 229

Forrest, John and Elizabeth Belfore, Dec. 25, 1761. p. 223

Forrest, Philip and Mary Calles, Nov.___, 1754. p. 220

Forster, Isaac and Miss Elizabeth Hodges, Feb. 11, 1773. License. p.230

Foster, Christopher and Mary Forrest, Aug. 6, 1776. Banns. p. 233

Foster, Francis and Alice Miller, Jan. 4, 1767. p. 226

Foster, George and Ann Glascock, July 17, 1763. p. 224

Foster, Joel and Mary Degge, Mar. 17, 1767. License. p. 226

Foster, Joshuah and Elizabeth Gayle, Aug. 28, 1753. p. 219

Foster, Joshua and Sarah Foster, Nov. 3, 1776. Banns. p. 233

Foster, Josiah and Caty Gayle, Oct. 14, 1751. p. 218

Foster, Peter and Ann Hall, Oct. 27, 1776. Banns. p. 233

Foster, Robert and Judith Miller, Mar. 26, 1769. p. 227

Foster, Thomas and Mary Alman, Jan. 22, 1750, by Rev. Richard Locke. Banns. p. 217

Foster, William and Betty Jordan Hall, Oct. 30, 1773. Banns. p. 230

Foster, _____ and _____ Thomas, Oct. 26, 1753. p. 219

Fowler, John of Fairfax and Ann Lilly of this Parish, July 20, 1776. Banns. p. 233

G

Gayle, George and Susannah Gayle, Mar. 17, 1768. p. 227

Gayle, Hunley and Lucy Gayle, July 11, 1777. Banns. p. 234

Gayle, James and Judith Gayle, Feb. 21, 1757. p. 221

Gayle, John and Susannah Davis, Sept. 12, 1758. License. p. 222

Gayle, John and Sarah Gayle, Sept. 22, 1763. License. p. 224

Gayle, Joseph and Elizabeth Morgan, Nov. 30, 1769. p. 227

Gayle, Mathew and Sukey Billups, May 3, 1753. p. 219

Gayle, Matthew and Susannah Boram, Oct. 5, 1758. p. 222

Gayle, Robert and Sarah Gayle, _____1768. License. p. 226

Gayle, Thomas and _____ce Gayle, Dec. 15, 1763. p. 224

Gibbons, William and Ann Blacknall, May 11, 1771, Thomas Feilde, Rector. License. p. 228

Glascock, Isaac and Ann Whiting Edwards, Nov. 2, 1768. p. 227

Glasscock, Abraham and Elizabeth Hudgin, Apr. 8, 1773. Banns. p. 230

Glasscock, John and Mary Williams, June __ 1753. p. 219

Gordon, John and Lucretia Singleton, Nov. 8, 1751. p. 218

Graves, John of Abingdon and Mildred Pritchard of this Parish, Sept. 25, 1776 Banns. p. 233

Green, George and Anna Hunley, June 24, 1774. Banns. p. 231

Green, James and Mary Westcomb, Mar. 12, 1774. Banns. p. 231

Green, James and Mary Jarratt, Apr. 9, 1775. Banns. p. 232

Green, John and Cathrine Hunley, Nov. 30, 1769. p. 227

Green, Robert and Elizabeth Respes, Aug. 26, 1764. License. p. 225

Green, William and Elizabeth Hunley, Dec. 25, 1765. p. 225

Grisset, James and Elizabeth _____, Aug. 25, 1762. p. 224

Gwyn, Humphry and Frances Peyton, Feb. 21, 1755. License. p. 220

Gwyn, John and Miss Dorothy Ransone, Feb. 6, 1773. License. p. 230

Gwyn, John and Ann Gwyn, Feb. 21, 1777. License. p. 234

Gwyn, Robert and Ann Ransone, Jan. 28, 1778. License. p. 234

Gwyn, Walter and Dorothy Reade, July __, 1763. License. p. 224

H

Hall, Edmond and Elizabeth Hill, Feb. 12, 1753. p. 219

Hardisty, Edward and Mary Merchant, Mar. 11, 1773. Banns. p. 230

Harper, James and Elizabeth Callis, Aug. 1, 1764. License. p. 225

Harris, Anthony and Dorothy Jarvis, Feb. 17, 1775. Banns. p. 232

Harris, James and Betty James, Jan. 10, 1766. License. p. 225

Harris, William and Susannah Putman, Feb. 22, 1756. p. 221

Hartswell, James and Betty Foster, Dec. 27, 1767. p. 226

Hayes, Hugh and Sarah Willis, Mar. 26, 1773. Banns. p. 230

Hayes, Thomas Jr. and Martha Hayes, Dec. 2_, 1751. p. 218

Hayes, _____ and Betty Blacknall, March 29, 1766. p. 225

Haywood, Elkin and Elizabeth Tomlinson, Jan. 5, 1775. Banns. p. 231

Hewel, Thomas and Sarah Nuthall, Aug. 9, 1774. Banns. p. 231

Hewell, William and Sarah Smithee, Jan. 1, 1756. p. 220

Hewil, Thomas and Elizabeth Terrier, Sept. 4, 1773. Banns. p. 230

Hilling, William and Lucy Peek, Dec. 8, 1769. p. 227

Hobdy, Brookes and Mary Elliot, Mar. 30, 1775. Banns. p. 232

Hodges, Richard and Mary King, Dec. 25, 1770, in Kingston Parish, Gloucester Co. by Rev. Thomas Baker. Banns. p. 228

Hudgen, Hugh and Mary Dawson, Nov. 10, 1768. p. 227

Hudgen, Lewis and Joice Steward, Aug. 24, 1765. p. 225

Hudgin, Alban and Elizabeth Weston, Jan. 17, 1762. p. 223

Hudgin, Ambrose and Anne Foster, Oct. 20, 1751. p. 218

Hudgin, Gabriel and Lucretia Hudgin, Nov. 27, 1751. p. 218

Hudgin, Holder and Mary Hunley, Jan. 27, 1769. p. 227

Hudgin, Humphry and Louisa Foster, Feb. 9, 1776. Banns. p. 233

Hudgin, James and Ann Jarvis, Sept. 16, 1761. p. 223

Hudgin, John and Ann Respes, Jan. 22, 1753. p. 219

Hudgin, John and _____, bet. Feb. & May 1764. p. 224

Hudgin, John and Mary Carney, Dec. 25, 1774. Banns. p. 231

Hudgin, Joshuah and Caty Hudgin, Feb. 6, 1757. p. 221

Hudgin, Kemp Whiting and Joyce Minter, Dec. 19, 1777. Banns. p. 234

Hudgin, Moses and Milly Bromly, May 13, 1767. p. 226

Hudgin, Moses and Elizabeth Soles, May 25, 1769. p. 227

Hudgin, Perrin and Sarah Minter, Oct. 18, 1774. Banns. p. 231

Hudgin, William and Johannah Degge, Nov. 30, 1756. p. 221

Hudgin, William and Mildred Brounly, Oct. 30, 1764. p. 225

Hudgin, William and Frances Morgan, Jan. 14, 1775. Banns. p. 231

Hudgin, William and Ann Peck, Mar. 10, 1765. p. 225

Hudgin, _____ and Elizabeth Burton, Apr. 10, 1757. p. 221

Hudgins, Aaron and Mary Callis, June 6, 1759. p. 222

Hudgins, Robert and Elizabeth Weskom, Dec. 22, 1770, in Kingston Parish, Gloucester Co., by Rev. Thomas Baker. Banns. p. 228

Huggart, James and Elizabeth Mason, July 17, 1765. p. 225

Hunley, Caleb and Jane Brown of Abingdon, Oct. __, 1758. p. 222

Hunley, Caleb and Elizabeth Smith, May 6, 1773. Banns. p. 230

Hunley, James and Mary Morgan, Dec. 24, 1764. p. 225

Hunley, James and Mary Biggs, May 12, 1766. p. 226

Hunley, John and An____ _____, June 12, 1762. p. 223

Hunley, John and Elizabeth Jarvis, Feb. 9, 1763. License. p. 224

Hunley, John and Mary Ayres, July 13, 1764. Banns. p. 225

Hunley, John and Parthenia Harris, Sept. 11, 1765. p. 225

Hunley, Joshua and Letitia Almun, Apr. 15, 1750, by Rev. Richard Locke. Banns. p. 217

Hunley, Matthis and Sarah Davis, Aug. 29, 1777. Banns. p. 234

Hunley, Philip and Elizabeth Dunbar, June __, 1767. p. 226

Hunley, Richard and Sarah Green, May 25, 1777. Banns. p. 234

Hunley, Robert and Joyce Gayle, June 30, 1774. Banns. p. 231

Hunley, Thomas and Sarah Lane, Nov. 21, 1754. p. 220

Hunley, Wilkinson and Rose Jarvis, Aug. 11, 1752. License. p. 219

Hunley, William and Elizabeth Hunley, Oct. 7, 1774. Banns. p. 231

Huntley, Henry and Mary Johnson, June 26, 1772. Banns. p. 229

Huntley, Matthew and Mary Turner, Mar. 8, 1772. Banns. p. 229

Hurst, Edward and Jane Hunley, Dec. 20, 1775. Banns. p. 232

Hurst, John and Elizabeth _____, July 22, 1759. p. 222

I

Iveson, Abraham of Ware Parish and Mary Dudley of this Parish, June 22, 1776. Banns. p. 233

J

Jackson, George and Mary Borten, Jan. 27, 1755. p. 220

Jackson, Thomas and Sarah Dagnall, July 21, 1776. Banns. p. 233

Jackson, William and _____ ton, Feb. __, 1762. p. 223

James, Mathias and Elizabeth Davis, Nov. 29, 1764. License. p. 225

James, Walter and Sarah Gayle, May 12, 1767. p. 226

Jarratt, William and Elizabeth Hodges, Apr. 5, 1775. Banns. p. 232

Jarret, Thomas and Elizabeth Fordham, Mar. 4, 1752. p. 219

Jarrot, John and Ann Ayres, Dec. 20, 1761. p. 223

Jarvice, William and Lucy Gowing, Jan. 22, 1750, by Rev. Richard Locke. Banns. p. 217

Jarvis, James and Lucy Davis, Dec. 26, 1774. Banns. p. 231

Jarvis, John and Sarah Jarvis, Nov. 12, 1774. Banns. p. 231

Jarvis, John and Mary Baxter, May 25, 1775. Banns. p. 232

Jarvis, Lindsey and Elizabeth Dixon, Nov. 6, 1772. Banns. p. 229

Jerrel, William and Jane Harris, Dec. 14, 1749, by Rev. Richard Locke. Banns. p. 217

Jervis, Francis and Elizabeth Christian, Dec. 25, 1769. p. 227

Jervis, Francis and Susanna Hill, Oct. 28, 1773. Banns. p. 230

Johnson, Hugh and Mary Brown, July 31, 1773. Banns. p. 230

Johnson, John and Judith Lucas, Oct. 30, 1756. p. 221

Johnson, Thomas and Jane Morgan, Dec. 9, 1749, by Rev. Richard Locke. Banns. p. 217

Johnson, Thomas and Mary Morgan, Oct. 27, 1752. p. 219

Johnston, John and Ann Peade, Aug. 13, 1775. License. p. 232

Jones, Edward Simmonds and Ann Billups, May 16, 1776. Banns. p. 233

Jones, James and Dorothy Cary, May 18, 1771, Thomas Feilde, Rector. License. p. 228

Jones, Thomas and Ann Hunley, Aug. 5, 1762. p. 224

Jones, Thomas and Mary Brookes, May 12, 1763. License. p. 224

Jones, William and Ann Iveson of Ware, Jan. 9, 1759. License. p. 222

K

Karr, Andrew and Ann Sadler, Jan. 3, 1755. p. 220

Kemp, William and Martha Dudley, Sept. 23, 1763. p. 224

Keys, Edward and Caty Williams, Mar. 18, 1775. Banns. p. 232

Keys, Howard and Susanna Treacle, Oct. 27, 1774. Banns. p. 231

King, John and Mary Hodges, May 8, 1766. No License to be had 20/ p.226

King, Thomas and Elizabeth Hodges, Oct. 21, 1770, in Kingston Parish, Gloucester Co. by Rev. Thomas Baker. Banns. p. 228

Knight, Henry and Elizabeth Millar, July 29, 1755. p. 220

Knight, Richard and Elizabeth Gayle, Oct. 19, 1752. p. 219

L

Lambeth, Merideth and Frances Bernard, Oct. 31, 1761. License. p. 223

Landom, William and Mary Angel, Jan. 11, 1771 by Thomas Feilde, Rector. Banns. p. 228

Lewis, Christopher and Caty Peed, Dec. 25, 1766. p. 226

Lewis, John and Elizabeth Poole, Sept. 14, 1773. Banns. p. 230

Lewis, Robert and Elizabeth Hudgins, Apr. 15, 1770, in Kingston Parish, Gloucester Co. by Rev. Thomas Baker. Banns. p. 228

Lewis, Thomas and Elizabeth Green (Ju^r), Dec. 1, 1751. License. p. 218

Lewis, Thomas and Anna Thomas, Apr. 14, 1775. Banns. p. 232

Little, John and Susannah Hunley, May 4, 1767. p. 226

Longest, Joshuah and Betty Edwards, Feb. 3, 1753. p. 219

Longest, Thomas and Ann Hudgin, Dec. 13, 1772. Banns. p. 229

Lowry, William and Mary Terrier, June 1, 1766. No License on Account
    of Stamp 20/   p. 226

Lucas, William and Mary Blacknall, Dec. 12, 1772. License. p. 229

Lyell, Jonathan and Mary Davis, March 8, 1761. License. p. 223

Lyl(e), John and Mary Cray, Dec. 10, 1776. Banns. p. 233

M

McDougal, Daniel of the Parish of Abingdon, Gloucester County and
    Elizabeth Johnson of this Parish, June 26, 1773. Banns. p. 230

Machen, John and Mary Boram, Dec. 22, 1767. p. 226

Machen, Samuel and Ann Thomas, Apr. 21, 1763. p. 224

Maggs, Thomas and Mary Sculley, Oct. __, 1753. p. 219

Mason, Thomas and Elizabeth Thomas, Aug. 22, 1774. Banns. p. 231

Massenburgh, Robert and Catharine ___pkins, Nov. 3, 1763. License. p.224

Mayo, John and Mary Tabb, Dec. 7, 1755. License. p. 220

Mayo, Joseph and Martha Tabb, Sept. 3, 1761. License. p. 223

Meggs, John and Judith Fordom, June 17, 1758. p. 222

Meggs, John and Sarah Bush, Feb. 28, 1767. p. 226

Merchant, Daniel and Ann Winder, Dec. 26, 1771 by Thomas Feilde, Rector.
    Banns. p. 229

Merchant, Edmond and Elizabeth Adams, Nov. 22, 1767. p. 226

Merchant, Elisha and Easter Merchant, Dec. 24, 1766. p. 226

Merchant, Richard and Ann Dawson, Feb. 12, 1763. p. 224

Merchant, William and Frankey Elliot, Dec. 22, 1768. License. p. 227

Millar, Thomas and Dorothy Matthews, Nov. 21, 1758. License. p. 222

Miller, Isaac and Elizabeth Hudgin, Dec. 23, 1762. p. 224

Miller, James and Ann Brounley, March 13, 1763. p. 224

Miller, Francis and Franky Callis, Jan. 14, 1775. Banns. p. 231

Miller, Francis and Averilla Degge, Oct. 6, 1776. Banns. p. 233

Minter, Anthony and Catherine Brounley, Dec. 19, 1777. Banns. p. 234

Minter, William and Mary Redman, Apr. 1, 1774. Banns. p. 231

Mintor, James and Ann Williams, Nov. 24, 1767. p. 226

Mintor, John and Ann Miller, Dec. 31, 1766. p. 226

Mitchel, Edmond and _____ Keeble, Jan. 28, 1762. License. p. 223

Mitchel, _____ and Joice Minter, Oct. 16, 1753. p. 219

Montgomery, David and Ann Hudgin, July 3, 1765. p. 225

Morgan, James and Elizabeth Forrest, Feb. 19, 1753. p. 219

Morgan, Mark and _____ _____ion, Feb. 3, 1762. p. 223

Morgan, Richard and Ann Bridge, Aug. 30, 1768. p. 227

Morgan, William and Ann Crawley, June 26, 1763. p. 224

Morris, James of Ware and Anna Fitzsimmons of Kingston, Oct. 12, 1770, in Kingston Parish, Gloucester Co. by Rev. Thomas Baker. Banns. p.228

Morris, John and _____, Feb. __1764. p. 224

Mullins, James and Mary Mintor, Feb. 14, 1763. p. 224

N

Nason, John and Hannah Jones, May 22, 1752. License. p. 219

Neale, Thomas and Judith Breedlove, Mar. 28, 1752. p. 219

Nuttall, John and Sarah Blacknall, March 5, 1763. License. p. 224

O

Oliver, Gravely and Judith Brown, Sept. 16, 1758. p. 222

Oliver, Gravely and Judith Respess, Dec. 7, 1770, in Kingston Parish, Gloucester Co., by Rev. Thomas Baker. Banns. p. 228

Owen, Edmond and Elizabeth Peed, Aug. 20, 1753. p. 219

Owen, William and Susannah Hall, Feb. 27, 1761. p. 223

P

Pallister, John and Mary King, Mar. 27, 1776. Banns. p. 233

Palmer, Nathaniel and Lucy Reade, Dec. 30, 1762. License. p. 224

Paris, Elisha and Elizabeth Roberts, Feb. 17, 1759. p. 222

Parrot, John and Sally Hudgin, June 14, 1761. p. 223

Parrot, Joseph and Ann Wake of Middlesex, Apr. 20, 1769. (Certificate). p. 227

Parrot, Michael and Ann Pallister, Apr. 9, 1757. p. 221

Parrot, Richard and Susanah Flippin, Jan. 8, 1762. p. 223

Parrot, Robert and Elizabeth Morgan, July 6, 1758. p. 222

Parrot, Robert and Mary Quin, July 10, 1761. p. 223

Parsons, James and Catherine Miller, Jan. 2, 1772. Thomas Feilde, Rector. License. p. 229

Peade, James and Sarah Owen, Jan. 5, 1775. Banns. p. 231

Peade, Lewis and Mary Williams, Jan. 13, 1775. Banns. p. 231

Peade, Thomas and Susanna Peak, Apr. 14, 1774. Banns. p. 231

Peake, Thomas and Dorothy Hudgin, Dec. 7, 1775. Banns. p. 232

Peed, Philip and Elizabeth Willis, July 22, 1759. p. 222

Peed, Philip and Dorothy Shipley, May 6, 1764. p. 225

Perkins, Whitney and Ann Miller, Feb. 15, 1770. p. 227

Perrot, George and Lucy Longest, May 17, 1772. Banns. p. 229

Perrot, John and Elizabeth Buchannan, July 25, 1773. Banns. p. 230

Peterson, Peter and Margaret Peed, Apr. 18, 1768. p. 227

Pew, William and Johannah Minter, Sept. 28, 1753. p. 219

Pied, James and Priscilla Hunley, Sept. 17, 1753. p. 219

Pigot, Galen and Frances Bernard Gayle, Dec. 24, 1775. Banns. p. 232

Plummer, George and Margaret Hayes, Aug. 25, 1768. License. p. 227

Pointer, Henry of Ware and Mary Tompkins of Kingston, Oct. 5, 1770 in Kingston Parish, Gloucester Co. by Rev. Thomas Baker. License. p. 228

Pointer, Seth and Mary Davis, Dec. 1, 1761. License. p. 223

Pool, Robert and Susanah Respes, Dec. 11, 1751. p. 218

Poole, Thomas and Elizabeth Hodges, Apr. 13, 1753. p. 219

Powell, John and Elizabeth Davis, July 13, 1761. p. 223

Pressley, John and Mary Jarvis, June 12, 1765. p. 225

Price, (The Rev. Mr.) Thomas and Mrs. Mary Armistead, Sept. 15, 1765. License. p. 225

Pritchard, John and Dorothy Brown, Nov. 16, 1768. p. 227

Pritchard, John and Joyce Lucas, Oct.___, 1772. Banns. p. 229

Pritchard, John and Hannah Gayle, May 28, 1776. Banns. p. 233

Pritchet, Joseph and Lucretia Merchant, June 7, 1761. p. 223

Pugh, Elias and Susanna Forrest, Jan. 4, 1777. Banns. p. 234

Purnall, John and Elizabeth Willis, March 18, 1765. p. 225

Q

Quin, Peter and Mary Bernard, Aug. 16, 1755. p. 220

R

Ransom, Richard and Ann Whiting, Mar. 21, 1771. Thomas Feilde, Rector. License. p. 228

Ransone, Augustine and Catharine Hill, Apr. 18, 1752. p. 219

Read, John and Judith Plummer, May 16, 1769. License. p. 227

Reade, Gwyn and *Harry* Ann Whiting, June 5, 1766. No Lic. on account of Stamp 20/   p. 226

Reade, James and Sarah Tompkins, Sept. 6, 1765. License. p. 225

Reaves, Robert and Jean Kees, Jan. 5, 1756. p. 220

Respes, Richard and Lucy Gayle, Feb. 14, 1756. p. 221

Respes, Thomas and Elizabeth Flippin, Apr. 2, 1761. p. 223

Respes, Thomas and Ann Curtis, Feb. 10, 1767. p. 226

Reynolds, John and Dorothy Stedder, Aug. 31, 1768. p. 227

Reynolds, William and Caty Pleacy, June 20, 1765. p. 225

Robbins, Alban and Elizabeth Williams, Sept. 23, 1762. p. 224

Robbins, Alban and Anna White, Jan. 17, 1766. p. 225

Robbins, Peter and Elizabeth Lewis, Sept. 10, 1765. p. 225

Robbins, Williams and Mary Lewis, Dec. 25, 1765. p. 225

Robins, William and Sarah Davis, July 21, 1777. Banns. p. 234

Robinson, Henry and Johannah Brookes, Nov. 7, 1765. License. p. 225

Rogers, John and Jane Bagas, Mar. 31, 1771. Thomas Feilde, Rector. Banns. p. 228

Rogers, Thomas and Ann Wilson, Dec. 23, 1771. Thomas Feilde, Rector. Banns. p. 229

Royston, Robert of Caroline and Rhoda Elliot of this Parish, Apr. 25, 1771. Thomas Feilde, Rector. License. p. 228

S

Sadler, Robert and Sarah Jarrot, July 4, 1756. p. 221

Sadler, Thomas and Mary Banks, Jan. 15, 1772. Banns. p. 229

Sadler, William and Ann Banks, Apr. 17, 1768. p. 227

Sampson, John and _____ _____iggs, Jan. 28, 1762. p. 223

Sampson, Thomas and Joyce Davis, Oct. 20, 1770, in Kingston Parish, Gloucester Co. by Rev. Thomas Baker. Banns. p. 228

Saunders, John and Mildred Saunders, Oct. 17, 1776. Banns. p. 233

Saunders, Thomas and Ann Davis, Feb. 27, 1773. Banns. p. 230

Sellers, Thomas and Ann Trikle, Oct. 14, 1755. p. 220

Shackelford, Benjamin and Miss Martha Jones, Dec. 24, 1770, in Kingston Parish, Gloucester Co. by Rev. Thomas Baker. License. p. 228

Shipley, Joseph and _____ _____, Apr. 16, 1762. p. 223

Shipley, Ralph and Joice Beard, Feb. 17, 1755. p. 220

Simmons, William and Anne Green, Oct. 29, 1769. p. 227

Singleton, Anthony and Ann Smith, Nov. 19, 1754. p. 220

Singleton, Henry and Letitia Hunly, Feb. 16, 1753. p. 219

Smith, James of Maryland and Elizabeth Lilly of this Parish, Nov. 14, 1771.
    Thomas Feilde, Rector. License. p. 228

Smith, Peter and Bathsheba Foster, Nov. 19, 1754. p. 220

Smith, (Capt.) Thomas and Ann Plater, Dec. 26, 1771. Thomas Feilde, Rector.
    License. p. 229

Smith, William and Bathseba Forster, Feb. 24, 1773. Banns. p. 230

Soper, John and Joyce Dixon, Dec. 21, 1771. Thomas Feilde, Rector. Banns.
    p. 229

Spencer, Robert and Sally Hayes, Jan. 3, 1767. p. 226

Sprat, James and Sarah Willis, Oct. 14, 1752. p. 219

Stedder, John and Ann Hunley, Mar. 4, 1773. Banns. p. 230

Stedder, Thomas and Susanna Callis, Mar. 11, 1771. Thomas Feilde, Rector.
    Banns. p. 228

Steward, James and Mary Degge, Apr. 1, 1766. p. 226

Steward, _____es and _____ _____, Feb. 20, 1766. p. 225

Stewart, John and Margaret Gale, June 16, 1771. Thomas Feilde, Rector.
    Banns. p. 228

Stubberfield, Thomas and Miss Johannah Merchant, Dec. 3, 1773. License.
    p. 230

Summers, John and Mary Fordam, Nov. 4, 1766. p. 226

Summers, Richard and Sarah Kees, July 8, 1759. p. 222

Summers, Richard and Margaret Welch, Nov. 27, 1761. p. 223

Summers, Richard and Betty Sadler, Dec. 23, 1774. Banns. p. 231

T

Tabb, Humphry Foye and Mary Peyton, Nov. 24, 1756. License. p. 221

Tabb, John and Frances Bird, daughter of Sir John Peyton Bird, Feb. 17, 1770
    (Guineas) License. p. 227

Tabor, Joseph and Martha Williams, Jan. 2, 1776. Banns. p. 233

Taylor, John and Joice Pleacy, July 21, 1765. p. 225

Terrier, Philip and Dilly Hudgin, June 2, 1775. Banns. p. 232

Thomas, George and Johanna Lewis, Dec. 26, 1775. Banns. p. 232

Thomas, James and Sarah Foster, Mar. 23, 1755. p. 220

Thomas, Mark and Mildred Davis, Oct. 12, 1770, in Kingston Parish, Gloucester Co. by Rev. Thomas Baker. Banns. p. 228

Thomas, Morgan and Elizabeth Davis, July 7, 1761. p. 223

Thomas, William and Judith Armistead, Aug. 13, 1764. p. 225

Thornton, Sterling and Ann Cary, Nov. 30, 1769. p. 227

Throgmorton, Mordecai and Mary Peyton, Dec. 11, 1773. License. p. 230

Tompkins, John and _____ Guess, Feb. __, 1764. License. p. 224

Tomkins, Samuel and Mary Tomkins, Apr. 9, 1753. p. 219

Treacle, John and Susanah Forrest, June 10, 1759. p. 222

Treacle, William and Elizabeth Dawson, Jan. 1, 1756. p. 220

Turner, George and Ann Ayers, July 8, 1750 by Rev. Richard Locke. Banns. p. 217

Turner, John and Elizabeth Hudging, Sept. ___, 1755. p. 220

Tyrrell, Michael and Susanna Foster, May 9, 1773. Banns. p. 230

W

Walker, Thomas and Elizabeth Debnam, Aug. 20, 1761. License. p. 223

Ward, Thomas and Clare Longest, Apr. 3, 1773. Banns. p. 230

Washington, Thacker (Gent.) and Miss Harriet Peyton, Oct. 12, 1776. License. p. 233

Waters, Francis and Elizabeth Rice, June 5, 1759. p. 222

Watson, John and Hannah Tabor, Feb. 6, 1776. Banns. p. 233

Weat, Peter and Sarah Billups, Jan. 30, 1756. p. 221

West, Benjamin and Mrs. Margaret Cary, Nov. 25, 1749, by Rev. Richard Locke. License. p. 217

Weston, John and Judith Steward, Oct. 20, 1755. p. 220

Weston, Major and Frances Forrest, _____ 1752. p. 218

White, Edward and Pemmy Singleton, Feb. 6, 1778. License. p. 234

White, James and Hannah Johnson, Dec. 25, 1751. p. 218

White, James and Mary White, Jan. 31, 1778. Banns. p. 234

White, John and Joice Callis, Dec. 30, 1764. p. 225

White, John and Ann Elliott, Jan. 3, 1772. License. p. 229

White, Richard and Mary White, Apr. 24, 1756. p. 221

White, William and Dorothy Davis, Feb. 3, 1775. Banns. p. 232

Whiting, Henry and Humphry Frances Toye, Nov. 11, 1762. License. p. 224

Whiting, Matthew and Martha Peyton, Nov. 22, 1751. License. p. 218

Whiting, Matthew and Elizabeth Toye, Feb. 26, 1763. License. p. 224

Wilkins, William of the Town _____ and Joyce Hunley (widow) of this Parish, _____, 1771. Thomas Feilde, Rector. p. 228

Williams, Daniel and Elizabeth Ducket, Aug. 26, 1756. p. 221

Williams, Francis and Elizabeth Cray, Oct. 5, 1772. Banns. p. 229

Williams, John and Sarah Rice, Nov. 25, 1754. p. 220

Williams, William and Abigail Tomolin, Apr. 26, 1763. p. 224

Williams, William and Elizabeth Crawford, Apr. 8, 1776. Banns. p. 233

Willis, Henry and Nancy Knight, May 6, 1770, in Kingston Parish, Gloucester County by Rev. Thomas Baker. Banns. p. 228

Willis, James and Hannah Foredom, June 15, 1766. p. 226

Willis, James and Sarah White, Jan. 26, 1755. p. 220

Willis, John and Jane _____, Dec. __, 1755. p. 220

Willis, John and Mary Foster, Aug. 17, 1775. Banns. p. 232

Willis, Thomas and Ann Younger, Nov. 18, 1751. p. 218

Willis, Thomas and Joyce Gowing, Dec. 18, 1756. p. 221

Willis, William and Ann Keys, Jan. 26, 1775. Banns. p. 232

Willis, William and Mary Green, Aug. 8, 1770, in Kingston Parish, Gloucester County by Rev. Thomas Baker. Banns. p. 228

Wilson, John and Catherine Rice, Aug. 8, 1775. Banns. p. 232

Wil____, William and Mrs. Sarah Billups (widow), Dec. 1, 1776. License. p. 233

Windor, Thomas and Elizabeth Beard, Feb. 16, 1755. p. 220

Wise, Abel and Ann Fitchett, Apr. 27, 1776. Banns. p. 233

Wi____, Thomas and _____ Davis, 1764 (bet. Feb. & May). p. 224

Wooden, George and Sarah Hunley, _____, 1752. p. 218

Wren, Kilbe and Elizabeth Degge, June 21, 1764. License. p. 225

Wright, William and Priscilla Gowing, Aug. 7, 1767. License. p. 226

    The last name of the male was not legible on the following marriages:

_____, William and Elizabeth Boswell, Dec. 22, 1776. Banns. p. 233

_____, James and Elizabeth Harris, Jan. 22, 1775. Banns. p. 231

_____, William and Sarah Powel, Jan. 21, 1775. Banns. p. 231

_____, Armistead and _____ _____, Sept. 25, 1763. p. 224

BIRTHS AND BAPTISMS

Adams, Mary, daughter of Zechariah and Ann. Born March 12 and Baptized April 9, 1775. p. 159

Adams, Stephen, son of Zechariah and Nancy. Born February 1 and Baptized February 27, 1774. p. 156

Amiss, Lucy, daughter of William and Ann Amiss. Born July 8 and Baptized August 15, 1762. p. 23

Anderson, Edward, son of Edward and Frances. Born March 26 and Baptized May 1, 1757. p. 14

Anderson, John, son of William and _____. Born January 22, 1750. p.103

Anderson, _____, son of Edward and Francess. Baptized ____, 1755. p. D

Anderton, Benjamin, son of William and Jane. Born July 2, and Baptized August 1, 1773. p. 154

Anderton, Dicky, son of John and Mary. Born October 9 and Baptized October __, 1771. p. 39

Anderton, Dorothy, daughter of Mark and Mary. Born May 1 and Baptized June 16, 1765. p. 28

Anderton, Elizabeth, daughter of William and Jane. Born January 30 and Baptized April 5, 1771. p. 39

Anderton, George, son of Mark and Mary. Born December __, 1770 and Baptized February 3, 1771. p. 38

Anderton, Isaac, son of Mark and Mary. Born May 27 and Baptized June 28, 1767. p. 32

Anderton, Isaac, son of William and Jane. Born March 18 and Baptized April 23, 1775. p. 159

Anderton, John, son of Mark and Mary. Born March 24 and Baptized May 9, 1762. p. 22

Anderton, John, son of William and _____. Born January 22, 1750. p. 103

Anderton, Joseph, son of William and Jane. Born January 25 and Baptized
March 5, 1769. p. 35

Anderton, Mary, daughter of John and Mary. Born April 2, and Baptized
May 1, 1768. p. 33

Anderton, Mildred, daughter of William and Jane. Born July 3 and Baptized
August 9, 1767. p. 32

Anderton, Ralph, son of John and Mary. Born May 14 and Baptized June 20,
1762. p. 23

Anderton, Richard, son of William and Mary. Born May 6 and Baptized
May 27, 1759. p. 18

Anderton, Sarah Hunley, daughter of William and Mary. Born November 3
and Baptized December 14, 1777. p. 166

Anderton, Thomas, son of William and Jane. Born July 8 and Baptized
August 24, 1766. p. 31

Anderton, William, son of Mark and Mary. Born August 9 and Baptized
October 9, 1763. p. 26

Anderton, _____ge, son of William and Mary. Baptized February 9, 1755.
p. D

Angel, Jemmy, son of William and Mary. Born May 18, and Baptized June 30,
1765. p. 28

Angel, Josiah, son of William and Mary. Born October 19 and Baptized
November 23, 1760. p. 20

Angel, Marget, daughter of William and Mary. Born April 9 and Baptized
June 19, 1763. p. 25

Angel, Robert, son of William and Mary. Born August 21 and Baptized
October 17, 1756. p. 12

Angel, _____, daughter of John and Mary. (no dates given) p. B

Armistead, Ann, daughter of Robert and Catharine. Born September 12 and
Baptized October 17, 1756. p. 13

Armistead, Anna, daughter of John and Ann. Born April 1, and Baptized
April 16, 1769. p. 35

Armistead, Anna Cleve, daughter of William Armistead, Esq. and Mary.
Born _____, 1773 and Baptized November 28, 1773. p. 155

Armistead, Caty, daughter of Richard and Elizabeth. Born January 21 and
Baptized February 12, 1775. p. 158

Armistead, Dorothy Reade, daughter of George and Lucy. Born May 23 and Baptized July 2, 1775. p. 159

Armistead, Elizabeth, daughter of Richard and Betty. Born August 22 and Baptized September 12, 1773. p. 154

Armistead, Francis, son of Currel and Margaret. Born _____ 1772 and Baptized March 1, 1772. p. 40

Armistead, Judith Carter, daughter of William Armistead, Esq. and Mary. Born December 30, 1774 and Baptized January 20, 1775. p. 158

Armistead, Mildred, daughter of Robert and Caty. Born February 11 and Baptized May 9, 1762. p. 22

Armistead, Ralph, son of Richard and Elizabeth. Born May 4, and Baptized June 10, 1770. p. 37

Armistead, Robert, son of John and Ann. Born September 26, and Baptized October 24, 1773. p. 154

Armistead, Sarah, daughter of William Armistead, Esq. and Mary. Born February 22, and Baptized March 3, 1776. p. 161

Armistead, Susanna, daughter of Richard and Elizabeth. Born August 26, and Baptized September 22, 1776. p. 163

Armistead, William, son of William and Mary. Born _____ 1770 and Baptized October 26, 1770. p. 37

Assetin, _____, son of (Dr.) David and Elizabeth. Born November 2, and Baptized November 13, 1755. p. 11

Ayres, James, son of John and Johanna. Born November 2, and Baptized November 14, 1776. p. 163

B

Baker, Ann Elizabeth, daughter of John and Sarah. Baptized December 1, 1771. p. 151

Baley, John, son of Matthew and Elizabeth. Born February 12 and Baptized March 12, 1775. p. 158

Baley, Matthew, son of Matthew and Elisabeth. Baptized May 9, 1777. p.165

Baley, William, son of Robert and Elizabeth. Baptized August 25, 1776. p.163

Banks, Ann Smither, daughter of James and Elizabeth. Baptized June 16, 1776. p. 162

Banks, Isaac, son of John and Ann. Born December 27, 1765 and Baptized
    February 23, 1766. p. 29

Banks, Jemmy, son of James and Elizabeth. Born March 18 and Baptized
    April 26, 1772. p. 40

Banks, John, son of James and Elizabeth. Born March 9, and Baptized
    April 1, 1770. p. 36

Banks, Joshua, son of James and Elizabeth. Born March 24 and Baptized
    May 8, 1774. p. 156

Banks, Joshua, son of John and Ann. Born December 30, 1761 and Baptized
    February 14, 1762. p. 22

Banks, Josiah, son of John and Ann. Born August 18, _____. p. C

Banks, Joyce, daughter of John and Ann. Born April 11 and Baptized
    May 27, 1759. p. 17

Banks, Joyce, daughter of John and Elizabeth. Born February 13 and
    Baptized March 25, 1764. p. 27

Banks, Milly, daughter of John and Ann. Born May 24 and Baptized June 27,
    1756. p. 12

Barnet, Mary Marlow, daughter of Frances Barnet. Born _____ 1772 and
    Baptized January 10, 1773. p. 152

Barnet, William, Sp.son of Dorothy Barnet. Baptized April 23, 1775. p.159

Barnett, James, son of William and Johannah. Born March 15 and Baptized
    May 11, 1760. p. 19

Barnett, William, son of William and Johanna. Born October 26 and
    Baptized November 13, 1757. p. 15

Basset, Dolly, daughter of Richard and Mary. Born May 20 and Baptized
    June 12, 1768. p. 33

Basset, Dorothy, daughter of Richard and Mary. Born May 18 and Baptized
    June 20, 1762. p. 23

Basset, Elizabeth Hunley, daughter of William and Rachel. Born May 13
    and Baptized July 1, 1770. p. 37

Basset, Jesse, son of William and Rachel. Born November 30, 1773 and
    Baptized January 27, 1774. p. 155

Basset, John, son of William and Rachel. Born September 25 and Baptized
    November 21, 1762. p. 24

Basset, Judith, daughter of William and Rachel. Born February 12, and Baptized March 20, 1768. p. 33

Basset, Mary, daughter of William and Mary. Born January 20 and Baptized March 13, 1774. p. 156

Basset, Mary, daughter of William and Rachel. Born April 28 and Baptized May 28, 1758. p. 16

Basset, Thomas, son of William and Rachel. Born May 15 and Baptized June 16, 1776. p. 162

Basset, William, son of William and Rachel. Born August 18 and Baptized September 8, 1765. p. 29

Baxter, Mary, daughter of John and Elizabeth. Born November 28 and Baptized December 11, 1757. p. 15

Baxter, James, son of John and Elizabeth. Born June 8, 1756 and Baptized June 27, 1756. p. 12

Bayley, Mary, daughter of Robert and Elizabeth. Born January 22 and Baptized February 26, 1775. p. 158

Beard, _____, a bastard daughter of Ann Beard. Born May 1755 and Baptized July 13, ____. p. 11

Beard, John, son of John and Dorothy. Born April 19 and Baptized May 9, 1773. p. 153.

Beard, William Hudgen, son of John and Dorothy. Born June 10 and Baptized July 8, 1770. p. 37

Behtley, William, son of Richard and Mary. p. B

Bell, Peter, son of Peter and Elizabeth. Born May 23 and Baptized June 12, 1774. p. 156

Bell, _____, (first name torn) child of Peter and Elizabeth. Born August ____, 1777. p. 165

Bernard, James, son of Henry and Mary. Born July 16 and Baptized August 22, 1756. p. 12

Billups, Ann, daughter of John and Mary. Born January 16, 1759. p.17

Billups, Christopher, son of John and Ann. Born May 25 and Baptized July 3, 1773. p. 154

Billups, Christopher, son of Robert and Elizabeth. Born July 31 and Baptized October 9, 1763. p. 25

Billups, Elizabeth, daughter of John and Ann. Born November 14 and
    Baptized December 27, 1767. p. 33

Billups, Elizabeth, daughter of Robert and Ann. Born October 11, 1757. p.15

Billups, Elizabeth Cary, daughter of Robert and Elizabeth. Born ___1772
    and Baptized January 19, 1772. p. 40

Billups, George, son of Robert and Elizabeth. Born July 23 and Baptized
    August 25, 1776. p. 163

Billups, Hugh Gwyn, son of Robert and Sarah. Born November 8 and
    Baptized November 15, 1775. p. 160

Billups, John, son of John and Ann. p. A

Billups, John, son of Robert and Ann. Born March 22, 1756. p. 12

Billups, John, son of Robert and Elizabeth. Born September 28, 1759. p.18

Billups, Joseph, son of Humphry and Mary. Born September 11 and Baptized
    November 14, 1756. p. 13

Billups, Joyce, daughter of John and Ann. Born July 4, 1758. p. 16

Billups, Langley, son of Thomas and Mildred. Born February 14 and
    Baptized March 18, 1770. p. 36

Billups, Lucy, daughter of Humphry and Frances. Born January 6 and
    Baptized March 27, 1775. p. 159

Billups, Lucy, daughter of Thomas and Mildred. Born _____ 1776. p. 162

Billups, Robert, son of Robert and Elizabeth. Born April 25 and Baptized
    June 8, 1774. p. 156

Billups, Rosanna, daughter of Thomas and Mildred. Born April 19 and
    Baptized May 7, 1773. p. 153

Billups, Sarah Gwyn, daughter of Robert and Sarah. Born August 20 and
    Baptized September 22, 1771. p. 39

Billups, Susanna, daughter of Robert and Elizabeth. Born January 31 and
    Baptized March 5, 1769. p. 35

Billups, Thomas Elliott, son of Thomas and Mildred. Born October 9 and
    Baptized November 20, 1774. p. 157

Billups, _____, daughter of Humphry and Mary. Baptized March __, 1755.
    p. D

Blacknall, Charles, son of Charles and Mary. Born January 10 and Baptized February 19, 1758. p. 16

Blacknall, Fanny, daughter of Elizabeth Marchant, whose father as she sayeth is Richard Blacknall. Born October 17 and Baptized December 18, 1763. p. 26

Blacknall, Mary, daughter of Charles and Mary. Born August 16 and Baptized September 12, 1755. p. 11

Blake, Mary, daughter of James and Ann. Born June 2 and Baptized July 5, 1772. p. 151

Blake, Mary, daughter of William and Elizabeth. Born March 12 and Baptized April 28, 1776. p. 162

Blake, Robert, son of William and _____. Born _____, 1773 and Baptized May 16, 1773. p. 153

Blake, Sarah, daughter of William and Dorothy. Born December 2, 1770 and Baptized February 24, 1771. p. 38

Blake, William, son of James and Mildred. Born February 19 and Baptized April 1, 1770. p. 36

Bloxham, Sarah, daughter of John and Sarah. Baptized May 5, 1771. p.151

Bohannan, Sarah Jordan, daughter of William and Mary. Born April 16 and Baptized June 18, 1775. p. 159

Bohannon, Esther, daughter of William and Mary. Born June 15 and Baptized July 18, 1762. p. 23

Bohannon, Judith, daughter of William and Mary. Born June 2 and Baptized July 1, 1764. p. 27

Bohannon, Nanny, daughter of William and Mary. Born July 18 and Baptized August 24, 1766. p. 31

Bohonnan, Joseph, son of William and Mary. Baptized April 3, 1773. p.152

Bond, Anna, daughter of William and Fanny. Born April __, 1762. p. 23

Boram, Benjamin, son of Edmund and Frances. Born February 10 and Baptized March 23, 1777. p. 164

Boram, Edmund, son of Edmund and Frances. Born May 5, 1769. p. 35

Boram, Franky, daughter of Edmund and Franky. Born June 4, and Baptized June 18, 1771. p. 39

Boram, John, son of Edmond and Frances. Born December 12, 1767. p. 33

31

Boram, Mary, daughter of John and Joanna. Born April 3 and Baptized May 19, 1776. p. 162

Boram, Nancy, daughter of John and Joanna. Born November 27, 1780. p. 171

Boram, Sally Jean, daughter of Edmund and Frances. Born September __, 1768 and Baptized November 15, 1768. p. 34

Boram, William Thornton, son of Edmund and Frances. Born March 17 and Baptized April 9, 1775. p. 159

Boram, _____ a child of Edward and Mary. p. A (Page A is torn)

Borum, Thomas Scott, son of Edmond and Elizabeth. Born November 26, 1794. p. 174

Boss, Hayes, son of Joseph and Sarah. Born February 7 and Baptized April 13, 1777. p. 164

Boss, John, son of Joseph and Susannah. Born April 18 and Baptized June 25, 1758. p. 16

Boss, Nanny, daughter of Joseph and Susannah. Born July 30 and Baptized September 9, 1764. p. 27

Boswell, Jane and Mary, Sp. twin daughters of Elizabeth Boswell. Born May 28 and Baptized May 29, 1776. p. 162

Boswell, John, son of Pangranparabo and Sarah. Born November 10 and Baptized December 12, 1756. p. 13

Boswell, Susanna, daughter of Robert and Lucretia. Born June 27 and Baptized July 24, 1768. p. 34

Boswell, Thomas, son of Robert and Sukey. Born January 6, and Baptized February 12, 1764. p. 26

Bramham, Mary, daughter of Richard and Sarah. Born July 6 and Baptized August 6, 1775. p. 160

Branham, Richard, son of Richard and Sally. Born May 10 and Baptized June 21, 1772. p. 151

Bridge, Elizabeth, daughter of William and Elizabeth. Born March 9 and Baptized May 11, 1760. p. 19

Bridge, John, son of Robert and Mary. p. B

Bridge, Polly, daughter of William and Ann. Born July 27, 1780. p. 171

Bridge, Ransom, a bastard son of Mary Bridge. Bron April __, 1757 and Baptized June 12, 1757. p. 14

Bridges, Elizabeth and John, Sp. son and daughter of Mildred Bridges.
Baptized November 19, 1776. p. 163

Bridges, Frances, Sp. daughter of Mildred Bridges. Born May 7 and
Baptized June 5, 1774. p. 156

Bridges, Sally Edwards, daughter of Richard and _____. Born ____, 1773
and Baptized May 16, 1773. p. 153

Bristow, Robert, son of Samuel and Mary. Born December 25, 1760 and
Baptized February 1, 1761. p. 21

Brookes, George, son of Thomas and Mary. Born May 8 and Baptized June 12,
1757. p. 14

Brookes, John, son of George and Susanna. Born May 8 and Baptized
November 15, 1767. p. 32

Brookes, Joyce Keeble, daughter of George and Susanna. Born May 30 and
Baptized June 30, 1762. p. 23

Brookes, Nancy, daughter of George and Susanna. Born January 20 and
Baptized March 13, 1774. p. 156

Brookes, Susannah, daughter of George and Susannah. Born April 21 and
Baptized June 16, 1765. p. 28

Brookes, Thomas, son of George and Susanna. Born February 26, 1757. p.14

Brookes, William, son of George and Susanna. Born October 12 and
Baptized December 9, 1770. p. 38

Brookes, _____her, son of Thomas and Mary. Baptized February 1_, 1755.
p. D

Brooks, Ann Smith, daughter of Richard and _____. Born April __, 1770
and Baptized April 11, 1770. p. 37

Brounley, Ann, daughter of Edward and Elizabeth. Born January 9 and
Baptized February 27, 1774. p. 156

Brounley, Ann, daughter of William and Elisabeth. Born April 27 and
Baptized May 18, 1777. p. 165

Brounley, Archibald, son of William and Elizabeth. Born September 15
and Baptized October 23, 1772. p. 151

Brounley, Archibald, son of William and Sarah. Born March 18 and
Baptized April 10, 1774. p. 156

Brounley, Archibald, son of Archibald and Sally. Born July 22 and
Baptized August 24, 1777. p. 165

Brounley, Foster, son of James and Elizabeth. Born November 2 and Baptized November 22, 1772. p. 152

Brounley, Frankey, daughter of Archibald and Sarah. Born December 4 and Baptized December 18, 1774. p. 158

Brounley, George, son of Archibald and Sarah. Born October 29 and Baptized November 10, 1771. p. 39

Brounley, James, son of Edward and Elizabeth. Born November 15, 1761 and Baptized January 10, 1762. p. 22

Brounley, Jesse, son of Archibald and Sarah. Born June 18 and Baptized July 14, 1776. p. 162

Brounley, John, son of Thomas and Abigail. Born March 17 and Baptized May 4, 1777. p. 164

Brounley, John, son of Archibald and Sarah. Born December 26 and Baptized December 31, 1772. p. 152

Brounley, Judith, daughter of Edward and Elizabeth. Born December 10 and Baptized December 31, 1772. p. 152

Brounley, Judith, daughter of William and Elizabeth. Born November 23 and Baptized December 4, 1774. p. 157

Brounley, Lucy, daughter of James and Elisabeth. Born November 5 and Baptized December 17, 1775. p. 160

Brounley, Lucy, daughter of James and Elisabeth. Baptized August 10, 1777. p. 165

Brounley, Robert, son of James and Margaret. Born September 10, and Baptized October 26, 1758. p. 16

Brounley, Sarah, daughter of William and Betty. Born January 15 and Baptized February 18, 1759. p. 17

Brounley, Thomas, son of Robert and Sarah. Born _____, 1773 and Baptized August 29, 1773. p. 154

Brounley, William, son of James and Sarah. Born August 1, and Baptized August 11, 1776. p. 163

Brounley, William, son of William and Sarah. Born June 22 and Baptized July 14, 1765. p. 29

Brounley, William, son of Augustine and Mary. Born March 25 and Baptized April 26, 1772. p. 40

Brounly, Ann, daughter of William and Sarah. Born March 28 and Baptized April 12, 1772. p. 40

Brown, Ann, daughter of George and Dorothy. Baptized April 9, 1776. p.162

Brown, Francis, son of William and Mary. Born January 28 and
   Baptized March 13, 1774. p. 156

Brown, George, son of Robert and Ann. Born _____, 1772 and Baptized
   January 31, 1773. p. 152

Brown, Jemmy Gayle, son of Robert and Ann. Baptized March 11, 1777. p.164

Brown, Judith Longest, daughter of William and Judith. Born November 25,
   1775 and Baptized January 14, 1776. p. 161

Brown, Richard Gayle, son of Robert and Ann. Born October 20 and
   Baptized December 4, 1774. p. 157

Brown, William, son of William and Judith. Born May 25 and Baptized
   June 26, 1768. p. 33

Brownley, Ann, daughter of Archibald and Ann. Born May 17 and Baptized
   June 22, 1760. p. 20

Brownley, Ann, daughter of Thomas and Abigail. Born January 14 and
   Baptized February 26, 1775. p. 158

Brownley, Ann, daughter of William and Sarah. Born August 19 and
   Baptized September 20, 1767. p. 32

Brownley, Archibald, son of Augustine and Mary. Born May 15 and
   Baptized October 4, 1767. p. 32

Brownley, Betty, daughter of Robert and Sarah. Born January 14 and
   Baptized February 26, 1775. p. 158

Brownley, Caty, daughter of William and Elizabeth. Born December 8, 1760
   and Baptized February 1, 1761. p. 21

Brownley, Dorothy, daughter of William and Sarah. Born September 6, 1763.
   p. 26

Brownley, Jesse, son of Archibald and Frances. Born March 2 and
   Baptized March 17, 1771. p. 38

Brownley, John, son of James and Margaret. Born February 25 and
   Baptized March 27, 1763. p. 25

Brownley, John, son of William and Sarah. Born November 11 and Baptized
   November 22, 1761. p. 22

Brownley, John, son of Archibald and Sarah. Born May 29 and Baptized
   November 15, 1767. p. 32

Brownley, Lucy, daughter of Edward and Elizabeth. Born March 27 and Baptized May 20, 1764. p. 27

Brownley, Martha, daughter of James and Elizabeth. Born May __, 1769 and Baptized June 25, 1769. p. 35

Brownley, Milley, daughter of William and Elizabeth. Born January 9 and Baptized February 21, 1768. p. 33

Brownley, Priscilla, daughter of William and Sarah. Born February 10 and Baptized February 18, 1770. p. 36

Brownley, Robert, son of Edward and Elizabeth. Born January 6 and Baptized February 13, 1763. p. 24

Brownley, Sarah, daughter of Edward and Elizabeth. Born March 22 and Baptized May 1, 1768. p. 33

Brownley, William and Joannah, son and daughter of James and Margaret. Born February 18, 1761. p. 21

Buckner, Mary, daughter of William and Elizabeth. Born April 24 and Baptized June 8, 1775. p. 159

Bum (Burn), Salley, daughter of Thomas and Alice. Born November 12, 1758. p. 17

Burge, Mary, daughter of William and Joyce. Baptized August 24, 1777. p.165

Burges, Davis, son of John and Mary. Born June 27 and Baptized August 11, 1765. p. 29

Burges, Elizabeth, daughter of John and Mary. Born April 8 and Baptized June 28, 1767. p. 32

Burges, Mary Alexander, daughter of John and Mary. Born July 12 and Baptized August 20, 1769. p. 36

Burges, Willoughby, son of John and Mary. Born February 5 and Baptized April 10, 1774. p. 156

Burgess, John, son of John and Mary. Born April 7 and Baptized June 9, 1771. p. 39

Burton, John, Sp. son of Mildred Burton. Baptized April 30, 1775. p. 159

Burton, John, son of William and Elizabeth. Born December 23 and Baptized February 18, 1759. p. 17

Burton, Mary <u>Charles</u>, daughter of Charles (deceased) and Ann. Born June 27 and Baptized August 9, 1777. p. 165

Burton, Nancy, Sp. daughter of Mildred Burton. Born _____, 1773 and
    Baptized April 4, 1773. p. 153

Bush, Dorothy Longest, daughter of George and Mary. Born January 2 and
    Baptized February 5, 1775. p. 158

B_____, Anna, daughter of Langley and Anna. p. A

C

Callice, Richard, son of Robert and Elizabeth. Born September 1, ___. p.C

Callis, Ann, daughter of Robert and Elizabeth. Born August 23 and
    Baptized September 24, 1775. p. 160

Callis, Ann, daughter of William and Susanna. p. A

Callis, Frankey, daughter of Robert and Elizabeth. Born May 29 and
    Baptized June 26, 1757. p. 14

Callis, Gabriel, son of Ambrose and Mary. Born August 1 and Baptized
    September 11, 1774. p. 157

Callis, George, son of James and Ann. Born October 2 and Baptized
    November 8, 1761. p. 22

Callis, James, son of James and Ann. Born October 28 and Baptized
    December 5, 1773. p. 155

Callis, James, son of William and Susanna. Born May 5 and Baptized
    June 7, 1761. p. 21

Callis, John, son of James and Ann. Born November 22, 1762 and
    Baptized January 30, 1763. p. 24

Callis, John, son of James and Ann. Born March 21 and Baptized
    April 20, 1777. p. 164

Callis, John, son of Ambrose and Mary. Born November 10, and Baptized
    December 6, 1772.

Callis, John, son of Robert and Elizabeth. Born April 10, and Baptized
    May 11, 1760. p. 20

Callis, Lewis, son of James and Elizabeth. p. A

Callis, Mary, daughter of James and Ann. Born March 23 and Baptized
    May 15, 1768. p. 33

Callis, Molly, daughter of Robert and Elizabeth. Born November 25 and
    Baptized December 18, 1763. p. 26

Callis, Nanny, daughter of Ambrose and Mary. Born December 10, 1769 and
Baptized January 21, 1770. p. 36

Callis, Richard, son of James and Ann. Born November 11, 1780. p. 171

Callis, Sally, daughter of Robert and Elizabeth. Born February 1 and
Baptized March 18, 1770. p. 36

Callis, William, son of James and Ann. Born May 11 and Baptized June 30,
1765. p. 28

Callis, William, son of William and Susanna. Born December 11, 1756. p. 13

Camp, Robert, son of Thomas and Mary. Born June 23 and Baptized August 1,
1756. p. 12

Campbell, Nanny, daughter of Alexander and Susanna. Born April 26 and
Baptized June 25, 1769. p. 35

Carey, Lucy, daughter of Dudley and Lucy. Born November __, 1776 and
Baptized December 27, 1776. p. 163

Carmines, Elvira Frances, daughter of Daniel and Hilligan. Born December 26,
1825. p. 180

Carney, Elizabeth West, daughter of William and Ann. Born June 16 and
Baptized July 2, 1775. p. 159

Carter, James, son of George and Jane. Born October 15, 1756. p. 13

Carter, Mary Edloe, daughter of William and Rebecca. Born March 5 and
Baptized April 23, 1773. p. 153

Cary, Elizabeth, daughter of John and Dorothy. Born January 28, 1758. p.16

Cary, John, son of John and Dorothy. Born May 9, 1761. p. 21

Chandler, Elly, daughter of William and Joyce. Born July 15, 1756. p. 12

Chandler, Lucy, daughter of William and Joyce. Born July 9, ____. p. C

Charley, Elizabeth, daughter of Robert and Frances. Born August 14 and
Baptized September 28, 1788. p. 173

Christian, Bailey, son of Israel and Martha. Born December 25, 1757 and
Baptized _____ 19, 1758. p. 15

Christian, George, Sp. son of Letitia Christian. Born May 27 and Baptized
June 30, 1776. p. 162

Christian, George Reade, son of Israel and Martha. Born August 20, 1755. p.11

Christian, Israel, son of Israel and Martha. Born August 30 and Baptized
    October 21, 1764. p. 27

Christian, John, son of Isral and Martha. Born October 16, 1761 and
    Baptized January 3, 1762. p. 22

Clare, (Fran)ces, daughter of John and Elizabeth. Baptized March 9, 1755.
    p. D

Clark, Joseph, son of Richard and Elizabeth. Born December 10, 1757 and
    Baptized February 5, 1758. p. 15

Clark, Thomas, son of William and Elizabeth. Born October 1 and
    Baptized November 15, 1777. p. 166

Clerk, (Tho)mas, son of Richard and Elisabeth. Born August 28 and
    Baptized October 5, 1755. p. 11

Coad, Mary, daughter of Michael and Hannah. Born February 7 and Baptized
    March 19, 1758. p. 16

Cooke, Mildred, daughter of Ignatius and Averilla. Born April 19 and
    Baptized May 17, 1771. p. 39

Corbin, Ann Lee, daughter of Gawin and Jane Byrd. Born ____ 1772 and
    Baptized June 7, 1772. p. 151

Corbin, Susannah, daughter of William and Annah. Born July 6 and
    Baptized August 4, 1771. p. 39

Crauley, Thomas, son of Abraham and Dorothy. Born August 18, ____ p. C

Crawley, William, son of Abraham and Elizabeth. p. B

Cray, James, son of James and Elizabeth. Born March 13 and Baptized
    April 9, 1775. p. 159

Cray, John, son of Richard and Ann. Born ____ 1773 and Baptized
    August 29, 1773. p. 154

Cray, Judith, daughter of James and Elizabeth. Born March 25 and
    Baptized April 7, 1773. p. 153

Cray, Mary, daughter of James and Mildred. Born June 21 and Baptized
    July 18, 1756. p. 12

Cray, Mary, daughter of John and Sarah. Born January 8 and Baptized
    January 15, 1775. p. 158

Cray, Mary James, daughter of John and Sarah. Born July 3 and
    Baptized July 28, 1776. p. 163

Cray, Milley, daughter of James and Mildred. Born January 17 and Baptized February 18, 1759. p. 17

Cray, William, son of James and Elizabeth. Born April 15 and Baptized May 20, 1770. p. 37

Cray, _____, son of Alexander and Mary. p. B

Cray, _____, child of James and Mildred. p. B

Creadle, _____, daughter of Benjamin and Elizabeth. p. B

Creedle, Benjamin, son of Benjamin and Elizabeth. Born June 17, 1757. p.15

Creedle, Betsey, daughter of Benjamin and Elizabeth. Born December 22, 1758 and Baptized January 21, 1759. p. 17

Creedle, William, son of Benjamin and Elizabeth. Born August 27 and Baptized October 5, 1755. p. 11

Creedle, William, son of Benjamin and Elizabeth. Born November 25, 1760. p.20

Culley, Elizabeth Dudley, daughter of Ralph and Mary. Baptized December 26, 1777. p. 166

Culley, George A., son of George and Mary. Born March 17, 1802. p. 176

Culley, Henry Loyd, son of George and Mary. Born October 29, 1805. p. 177

Culley, John L., son of George and Mary. Born June 28, 1800. p. 176

Culley, Judith, daughter of Christopher and Mary. Born January 6 and Baptized February 14, 1775. p. 158

Culley, Julian, daughter of George and Mary. Born November 25, 1803. p.176

Cully, Ann, daughter of Christopher and Mary. Born September 28 and Baptized October 24, 1773. p. 155

Cully, Elizabeth, daughter of Christopher and Mary. Born August 3 and Baptized September 6, 1767. p. 32

Cully, Elizabeth, daughter of Thomas and Mary. Born January 22 and Baptized February 20, 1757. p. 14

Cully, Mary, daughter of Robert and Judith. Born September 1 and Baptized October 17, 1756. p. 13

Curtis, Catherine, daughter of Edmund and Bridget. Born January 5 and Baptized February 16, 1773. p. 152

Curtis, Charles, son of John and Sarah. Born April 13 and Baptized May 11, 1777. p. 165

Curtis, James, son of John and Sarah. Baptized January 3, 1775. p. 158

D-

Dance, James, son of _____ and _____. Baptized November 12, 1775. p.160

Davis, Alice, daughter of James and Alice. Born November 11, 1764. p. 28

Davis, Armistead, son of Isaac and Rebecca. Baptized December 5,1773. p.155

Davis, Betty, daughter of Thomas and Hillegant. Born September 15 and Baptized October 23, 1763. p. 26

Davis, Billups Hudgin, son of James and Catharine. Born November 30, 1804. p. 176

Davis, Catherine and Hillegen, twin daughters of Isaac and Rebecca. Born December 14, 1776 and Baptized February 5, 1777. p. 164

Davis, Christopher, son of Christopher and Elizabeth. Born April 15, 1825 p. 180

Davis, Christopher, son of Thomas and Lucretia. Born June 1 and Baptized July 21, 1783. p. 172

Davis, Daniel, son of Edward and Mary. Born June 11, 1795. p. 174

Davis, Dickey, son of John and Elizabeth. Born June 3 and Baptized July 3, 1763. p. 25

Davis, Dolly, daughter of Edward and Sarah. Born June 8 and Baptized July 17, 1774. p. 157

Davis, Dorothy, daughter of John and Dorothy. Born July __, 1761. p.21

Davis, Edward, son of Edward and Mary. Born January 29, 1786. p. 172

Davis, Edward, son of Edward and Mary. Born April 6, 1793. p. 174

Davis, Edward, son of James and Alice. Born December 20, 1768. p. 34

Davis, Edward, son of Joseph and Lettice. Born March 8 and Baptized April 10, 1774. p. 156

Davis, Elizabeth, daughter of Edward and Sarah. Born October 17 and Baptized November 25, 1759. p. 19

Davis, Elizabeth, daughter of Edward and Sarah. Born July 13 and Baptized August 9, 1767. p. 32

Davis, Elizabeth, daughter of Isaac and Ann. Born May 14, 1769. p. 35

Davis, Elizabeth, daughter of John and Elizabeth. Born March 21 and Baptized May 4, 1766. p. 30

Davis, Elizabeth, daughter of Thomas and Lucretia. Born January 8 and Baptized February 18, 1770. p. 36

Davis, Elizabeth Burges, daughter of Christopher and Elizabeth H. Born April 12, 1817. p. 178

Davis, Elizabeth Degge, daughter of Edward and Francis. Born April 26 and Baptized May 23, 1773. p. 153

Davis, Elizabeth and Stephen, daughter and son of John and Dorothy. Born March 16, 1766. p. 30

Davis, Frances, daughter of Edward and Mary. Born July 11 and Baptized August 29, 1790. p. 173

Davis, Frances, daughter of John and Elizabeth. Born June 19 and Baptized July 23, 1769. p. 35

Davis, Frances, daughter of John and Dorothy. Born June 22 and Baptized July 3, 1774. p. 156

Davis, Humphry, son of James and Alice. Born May 18 and Baptized June 18, 1771. p. 39

Davis, Isaac, son of Isaac and Ann. Born May 9 and Baptized June 29, 1766. p. 30

Davis, James, son of Edward and Mary. Born January 28, 1788. p. 173

Davis, James, son of Edward and Sarah. Born January 24 and Baptized March 5, 1769. p. 35

Davis, James, son of James and Alice. Born November 16, 1758 (deceased). p.17

Davis, James, son of James and Ann. Born November 15 and Baptized December 15, 1776. p. 163

Davis, James, son of John and Elizabeth. Born December 26, 1759 and Baptized February 3, 1760. p. 19

Davis, James Hudgin, son of James and Catharine. Born September 25, 1802. p. 176

Davis, James Marshall, son of Christopher and Elizabeth H. Born February 11, 1820. p. 178

Davis, John, son of Edward and Mary. Born December 7, 1781. p. 171

Davis, John, son of Isaac and Ann. Born July 31 and Baptized August 21, 1757. p. 15

Davis, John, son of James and Alice. Born March 24, 1763. p. 25

Davis, Joseph, son of Edward and Sarah. Born January 25, 1766. p. 30

Davis, Leah, daughter of Edward and Mary. Born January 12, 1784. p. 171

Davis, Leah, daughter of James and Alice. Born February 19, 1757 (deceased) p. 14

Davis, Letitia Wren, daughter of Joseph and Lettice. Baptized December 17, 1775. p. 160

Davis, Lucy, daughter of John and Dorothy. Born April 13, and Baptized May 15, 1768. p.33

Davis, Lucy, daughter of Thomas and Lucretia. Born May 23 and Baptized June 28, 1788. p. 172

Davis, Mary, daughter of Edward and Sarah. Born June 8 and Baptized July 13, 1766. p. 30

Davis, Mary, daughter of John and Dorothy. Born August 6 and Baptized September 29, 1763. p. 26

Davis, Mary, daughter of Thomas and Susanna. Baptized November 17, 1776. p. 163

Davis, Martha Ann Jackson, daughter of Christopher and Elizabeth H. Born October 5, 1828. p. 180

Davis, Meredith, son of James and Alice. Born December 7, 1773 and Baptized February 2, 1774. p. 155

Davis, Nancy, daughter of Edward and Sarah. Born February 15 and Baptized March 19, 1758. p. 16

Davis, Nancy, daughter of Joseph and Lettice. Born February 18 and Baptized March 29, 1772. p. 40

Davis, Nancy Bailey, daughter of James and Catharine. Born March 20, 1800. p. 176

Davis, Paulina Frances, daughter of Christopher and Elizabeth H. Born April 24, 1815. p. 178

Davis, Philip, son of John and Dorothy. Born May 13 and Baptized May 27, 1759. p. 18

Davis, Ralph Armistead, son of Thomas and Catharine. Born July 26, 1799. p. 176

Davis, Sally, daughter of Edward and Sarah. Born July 10 and Baptized August 15, 1762. p. 23

Davis, Sarah, daughter of Edward and Sarah. Born ____, 1772 and Baptized January 15, 1772. p. 40

Davis, Sarah, daughter of John and Dorothy. Born February 26 and Baptized March 17, 1771. p. 38

Davis, Thomas, son of Edward and Francis. Born April 29, 1770. p. 37

Davis, Thomas, son of Edward and Sarah. Born January 20 and Baptized February 25, 1764. p. 26

Davis, Thomas, son of Isaac and Ann. Born February __, 1763 and Baptized April 10, 1763. p. 25

Davis, Thomas, son of James and Alice. Born December 31, 1760. p. 21

Davis, Thomas, son of Thomas and Hillegon. Born October 23 and Baptized November 25, 1759. p. 19

Davis, Thomas, son of Thomas and Lucrecia. Born April 10, 1790. p. 173

Davis, William, son of James and Ann. Baptized December 18, 1774. p.158

Davis, William, son of James and Alice. Born December 1 and Baptized December 15, 1766. p. 31

Davis, William, son of John and Dorothy. Born January 23 and Baptized February 6, 1757. p. 14

Davis, William, son of John and Elizabeth. Born December 12, 1756 and Baptized January 23, 1757. p. 13

Davis, William, son of John and Elizabeth. Born March 16, 1780. p.171

Davis, William, son of Joseph and Lettice. Born October 22 and Baptized December 2, 1777. p. 166

Davis, _____, child of Isaac and Ann. p. A

Davis, _____, son of John and Dorothy. p. D

Davis, _____, daughter of John and Dorothy. p. D

Davis, _____, child of James and Alice. Baptized 1755. p. D

Dawson, Ann, daughter of Samuel and Ann. Born January 19, 1760. p. 19

Dawson, Elizabeth, daughter of James and Mary. Born June 6 and Baptized July 11, 1773. p. 154

Dawson, Elizabeth, daughter of Leonard and Ann. Born July 3 and Baptized July 22, 1759. p. 18

Dawson, Leonard, son of Leonard and Ann. Born April 20 and Baptized June 3, 1764. p. 27

Dawson, Mary Booker, daughter of James and Mary. Baptized October 20, 1776. p. 163

Dawson, Robert Hudgin, son of Leonard and Ann. Baptized March 31, 1776. p. 162

Dawson, Thomas, son of Samuel and Ann. Born January 31 and Baptized February 19, 1758. p. 16

Dawson, Thomas, son of Leonard and Ann. Born October 7 and Baptized October 23, 1772. p. 151

Dawson, William Holder, son of Leonard and Ann. Born April 4 and Baptized May 9, 1762. p. 23

Deal, John, son of John and _____. Baptized June 16, 1776. p. 162

Dean, Rosanna Lilly, daughter of Josiah and Rosanna. Baptized March 10, 1776. p. 161

Degge, Ann, daughter of Anthony and Avarilla. Born September 8, and Baptized October 12, 1758. p. 16

Degge, Anthony, son of Joshua and Betty. Born May 20 and Baptized June 16, 1765. p. 28

Degge, Augustine, son of Joshua and Betty. Born July 15 and Baptized August 28, 1774. p. 157

Degge, Augustine, son of Augustine and Mary. Born April 29 and Baptized June 8, 1760. p. 20

Degge, Avarilla, daughter of Joshua and Caty. Born December 2, 1758 and Baptized February 4, 1759. p. 17

Degge, Bailey, son of Augustine and Mary. Born _____ 1772 and Baptized February 11, 1773. p. 152

Degge, Bathsheba, daughter of Augustine and Sarah. Born June 21 and Baptized August 15, 1762. p. 23

Degge, Charles, son of Joseph and Sarah. Born November 18 and Baptized December 16, 1764. p. 28

Degge, Christopher, son of William and Mary. Born February 25 and Baptized April 2, 1769. p. 35

Degge, David, son of Joshua and Betty. Born October 11 and Baptized November 13, 1768. p. 34

Degge, Elizabeth, daughter of Joseph and Sarah. Born January 13, and
    Baptized February 14, 1762. p. 22

Degge, Henry and John, twin sons of Joseph and Sarah. Born June 17
    and Baptized November 15, 1767. p. 32

Degge, Isaac, son of Augustine and Mary. Born April 25 and Baptized
    May 28, 1758. p. 16

Degge, Isaac, son of John and Ann. Born August 27 and Baptized
    September 8, 1776. p. 163

Degge, Isaac, son of Joshua and Betty. Born May 5 and Baptized
    July 8, 1770. p. 37

Degge, Isaac, son of William and Mary. Born November 3 and Baptized
    December 1, 1776. p. 163

Degge, James, son of Joseph and Sarah. Born February 8 and Baptized
    March 17, 1771. p. 38

Degge, Jesse, son of Augustine and Mary. Born May 21 and Baptized
    July 9, 1769. p. 35

Degge, Joel, son of Joshua and Betty. Born June 18 and Baptized
    August 11, 1776. p. 163

Degge, John, son of Augustine and Mary. Born September 24,____. p. C

Degge, John, son of Joshua and Betty. Born August 11 and Baptized
    October 16, 1772. p. 151

Degge, Joseph, son of Joseph and Sarah. Born September 21 and
    Baptized November 25, 1759. p. 18

Degge, Joshua, son of Augustine and Mary. Born July 12 and Baptized
    August 22, 1756. p. 12

Degge, Josiah, son of Augustine and Mary. Born February 14 and
    Baptized May 19, 1765. p. 28

Degge, Lauson, son of Anthony and Averilla. Born August 24 and
    Baptized September 22, 1764. p. 27

Degge, Lawson, son of John and Joyce. Born February 5 and Baptized
    April 12, 1776. p. 162.

Degge, Louisa, daughter of Joshua and Betty. Born February 25 and
    Baptized April 10, 1763. p. 25

Degge, Mary, daughter of Joel and Mary. Born July 14 and Baptized
    August 28, 1774. p. 157

Degge, Mary, daughter of Joshua and Betty. Born January 9 and Baptized
    February 22, 1767. p. 31

Degge, Molly, daughter of Anthony and Averilla. Born June 6 and Baptized
    July 5, 1761. p. 21

Degge, Rebecca, daughter of Joseph and Sarah. Born January 19 and Baptized
    February 20, 1757. p. 14

Degge, Sarah, daughter of Augustine and Mary. Born March 17 and Baptized
    May 17, 1767. p. 32

Degge, Simon, son of William and Mary. Born February 19 and Baptized
    March 12, 1775. p. 158

Degge, William, son of Josiah and Caty. Born December 18, 1760 and
    Baptized February 1, 1761. p. 21

Degge, _____, child of Augustine and Mary. p. B

Degg(e), _____, son of Joseph and Sarah. p. B

Dennis, Elizabeth Davis, daughter of James and Elizabeth. Baptized May 5,
    1771. p. 151

Dennis, William, son of James and Elizabeth. Born _____ 1773 and Baptized
    July 11, 1773. p. 154

Digges, Nancy, daughter of William and Mary. Born February 25 and Baptized
    April 24, 1773. p. 153

Dixon, Ann, daughter of William and Elizabeth. Born June 4 and Baptized
    July 8, 1775. p. 160

Dixon, John, son of John Dixon, Jr. and Elizabeth. Born _____ 1773 and
    Baptized December 11, 1773. p. 155

Dixon, Susanna, daughter of Tindsly and Lucretia. Born April 13 and Baptized
    May 9, 1762. p. 23

Dixon, Thomas, son of Rev. John Dixon and Lucy. Born December 26, 1760 and
    Baptized January 2, 1761. p. 21

Dixon, William, son of Rev. John Dixon and Lucy. Born October 12 and
    Baptized November 12, 1758. p. 17

Driver, Mary, a mylatto bastard, daughter of Susanna Driver. Born April 1761
    p. 21

Driver, Richard, Sp. son of Susanna Driver. Born May 10 and Baptized
    June 13, 1773. p. 154

Driver, William, son of William and Susannah. Born January 17, 1759. p. 17

Dudley, Ann Billups, daughter of George Alexander Dudley and Mary. Born March 27 and Baptized May 19, 1777. p. 165

Dudley, Armistead, son of Robert Ballard Dudley and Ann "of Ware Parish". Born January 27 and Baptized April 7, 1771. p. 39

Dudley, Charles, son of William and Rebecca. p. B

Dudley, George Alexander, son of George Alexander Dudley and Mary. Born March 22 and Baptized May 14, 1774. p. 156

Dudley, Mary, daughter of William and Sally. Born July 17 and Baptized August 15, 1772. p. 151

Dunlavy, Anthony, son of Anthony and Mary. Baptized December 10, 1775. p. 160

Dunlavy, William, son of William and Ann. Born February 19 and Baptized March 19, 1775. p. 158

Duplecy, Betsy, daughter of Charles and Amy. Born December 25, 1772 Baptized January 31, 1773. p. 152

Duplecy, Sarah, daughter of Charles and Ann. Born May 28 and Baptized June 19, 1774. p. 156

Dye, Richard, son of Richard and Suky. Born March 24 and Baptized April 30, 1775. p. 159

E

Eddens, Elizabeth, daughter of Samuel and Nancy. Born August __, 1773 and Baptized September 20, 1773. p. 154

Eddens, John, son of Dawson and Letitia. Born September 2 and Baptized October 29, 1769. p. 36

Eddens, Langley Billups, son of Dawson and Letitia. Born _____, 1772 and Baptized January 14, 1772. p. 40

Eddens, Lucy, daughter of John and Susannah. Born December 26, 1756 and Baptized January 3, 1757. p. 13

Eddens, Sarah, daughter of Dawson and Letitia. Born December 28, 1776 and Baptized February 9, 1777. p. 164

Eddens, Thomas Cary, son of Dawson and Letitia. Born October 7, and Baptized November 6, 1774. p. 157

Eddens, Thomas, son of Samuel and Ann. Born October 11 and Baptized October 25, 1771. p. 40

Ellis, Robert Evans, bastard son of Catherine Ellis. Born December __, 1770 and Baptized February 24, 1771. p. 38

Emerson, Peggy, daughter of John and Mary. Born March 10, 1796. p. 175

Enos, Robert, son of Francis and Sarah. Born March 5 and Baptized April 13, 1777. p. 164

Enos, Sarah, daughter of Francis and Sarah. Born March 22 and Baptized April 30, 1775. p. 159

Enos, William, son of Francis and Sary. Born September 11, 1780. p. 171

Evans, Betsey, daughter of Lewis and Judith. Born May 4 and Baptized May 11, 1773. p. 153

Evans, Franky, daughter of William and Lannas. Born March 4, 1781. p. 171

Evans, George, son of William and Anna. Baptized October 5, 1777. p. 166

Evans, William, son of William and Anna. Born January 10 and Baptized March 2, 1774. p. 156

F

Filyoung, (Geor)ge, son of George and Elizabeth. Born May __, 1755 and Baptized July 13, 1755. p. 11

Fichet, William, son of Daniel and Sarah. Born March 7 and Baptized April 5, 1760. p. 19

Fitchet, Daniel, son of Thomas and Ann. Born November 20, 1776 and Baptized January 23, 1777. p. 164

Fitchet, Joshua, son of Daniel and Sarah. Born March 12 and Baptized March 27, 1763. p. 25

Fitchet, Salathiel, son of Daniel and Sarah. Born June 12 and Baptized July 17, 1774. p. 157

Fitchet, Sarah, daughter of Thomas and Ann. Born April 1 and Baptized May 9, 1775. p. 159

Fitchet, Susanna, daughter of Daniel and Sarah. Born July 2 and Baptized August 7, 1768. p. 34

Fittchet, Daniel, son of Daniel and Sarah. Born August 30 and Baptized October 2, 1757. p. 15

Flippen, Thomas, son of Humphry and Sarah. Born August 24 and Baptized September 20, 1767. p. 32

Flippen, Armistead, son of Thomas and Dorothy. Born December 12, 1770 and
   Baptized February 6, 1771. p. 38

Flippen, Jenny, daughter of Thomas and Dorothy. Born February 10 and
   Baptized April 1, 1775. p. 159

Flippin, Machen, son of John and _____. Baptized January 8, 1775. p.158

Flippin, Nancy Davis, duaghter of Humphry and Mary. Born June 19 and
   Baptized July 3, 1776. p. 162

Flippin, Thomas, son of Thomas and Dorothy. Born May 29 and Baptized
   July 27, 1773. p. 154

Flucher, Ann, daughter of Thomas and Ann. Born March 10 and Baptized
   May 4, 1766. p. 30

Flucher, John, son of Thomas and Ann. Born February 18 and Baptized
   April 2, 1769. p. 35

Fordom, Edward, son of Edward and Margaret. Born July 26 and Baptized
   August 24, 1766. p. 31

Fordom, Elizabeth, daughter of Edward and Margaret. Born August 3 and
   Baptized September 4, 1768. p. 34

Forrest, Alice, daughter of John and Dorothy. Born March 30 and Baptized
   April 26, 1761. p. 21

Forrest, Ann, daughter of George and Ann. Born May 12 and Baptized
   October 4, 1767. p. 32

Forrest, Ann, daughter of John and Ann. Born January 5, and Baptized
   February 20, 1757. p. 14

Forrest, Betsy, daughter of George and Elizabeth. Born October 27, 1770.
   p. 38

Forrest, Dorothy, daughter of John and Dorothy. Born November 6 and
   Baptized December 14, 1777. p. 166

Forrest, Dorothy Elliott, daughter of Henry and Anna. Born May 8 and
   Baptized June 18, 1775. p. 159

Forrest, Edmund, son of John and Mary. Born August 25, 1755. p. 11

Forrest, Elizabeth, daughter of John and Dorothy. Born May 27 and
   Baptized July 4, 1773. p. 154

Forrest, Elizabeth Hunley, daughter of George and Mary. Born December 5,
   1780. p. 171

Forrest, George, son of George and Elisabeth. Born February 13 and Baptized March 23, 1777. p. 164

Forrest, George, son of George and Mary. Born May 8 and Baptized June 7, 1773. p. 153

Forrest, George, son of Philip and Mary. Born January 2 and Baptized February 19, 1758. p. 16

Forrest, Henry, son of Thomas and _____. Born January 8, 1749. p. 103

Forrest, James, son of George and Elizabeth. Born December 9, 1767 and Baptized January 10, 1768. p. 33

Forrest, Jesse, son of George and Mary. Born March 3 and Baptized March 26, 1775. p. 158

Forrest, John, son of George and Ann. Born May 21 and Baptized June 25, 1769. p. 35

Forrest, John, son of John and Dorothy. Born January 20 and Baptized March 11, 1763. p. 24

Forrest, John, son of Philip and Mary. Born May 9 and Baptized June 27, 1756. p. 12

Forrest, John, son of Thomas and Mary. Born January 14 and Baptized January 30, 1776. p. 161

Forrest, Joyce, daughter of George and Elizabeth. Born February 6 and Baptized March 10, 1765. p. 28

Forrest, Letitia Hayes, daughter of Henry and Anna. Born March 26 and Baptized May 7, 1773. p. 153

Forrest, Mary, daughter of John and Dorothy. Born February 25 and Baptized March 23, 1766. p. 30

Forrest, Mary, daughter of Philip and Mary. Born December 15, 1762 and Baptize March 30, 1763. p. 24

Forrest, Matthew, son of George and Mary. Born February 9 and Baptized March 3, 1771. p. 38

Forrest, Molly, daughter of George and Elizabeth. Born April 25 and Baptized June 5, 1774. p. 156

Forrest, Nancy, daughter of Philip and Mary. Born March 27 and Baptized May 11, 1760. p. 19

Forrest, Richard, son of George and Ann. Born February 3, 1759. p. 17

51

Forrest, Sally, daughter of George and Ann. Born October 15, 1762. p. 24

Forrest, Sarah, daughter of Philip and Mary. Born October 19 and Baptized November 3, 1765. p. 29

Forrest, Thomas, son of George and Ann. Born August 11, ____. p. C

Forrest, Thomas, son of Thomas and Mary. Born March 17 and Baptized April 20, 1777. p. 164

Forrest, _____m, son of John and Ann. Baptized February 23, 1755. p. D

Forrest, _____, daughter of George and Ann. p. B

Foster, Amelia, daughter of John and Rose. Born October 9 and Baptized November 23, 1760. p. 20

Foster, Ann, daughter of George and Ann. Born December 22, 1766. p. 31

Foster, Ann, daughter of Josiah and Caty. Born April 29 and Baptized June 25, 1769. p. 35

Foster, Betsey, daughter of Robert and Elizabeth. Born September 27 and Baptized October 24, 1773. p. 154

Foster, Betty, daughter of Joshua and Elizabeth. Born February 22 and Baptized April 8, 1764. p. 27

Foster, Betty, daughter of Josiah and Caty. Born December 14 and Baptized January 31, 1762. p. 22

Foster, Elisabeth, daughter of Joel and Mary. Born April 1 and Baptized May 19, 1777. p. 165

Foster, George, son of George and Ann. Born March 16 and Baptized April 8, 1773. p. 153

Foster, James, son of Francis and Alice. Born October 18 and Baptized November 5, 1775. p. 160

Foster, James, son of Richard and Susanna. Born December 15, 1759 and Baptized February 17, 1760. p. 19

Foster, James, son of Robert and Elizabeth. Born December 11, 1770 and Baptized January 6, 1771. p. 38

Foster, Jesse, son of Joel and Elizabeth. Born June 6 and Baptized November 15, 1767. p. 32

Foster, Jesse Johnson, son of Joshua and Elizabeth. Born June 4 and Baptized July 18, 1773. p. 154

Foster, Joel, son of John and Rose. Born August 15 and Baptized
    September 26, 1762. p. 23

Foster, John, son of Isaac and Elisabeth. Born June 6 and Baptized
    July 16, 1775. p. 160

Foster, John, son of Joshua and Elizabeth. Born June 30 and Baptized
    August 20, 1761. p. 21

Foster, John, son of Josiah and Caty. Born January 6 and Baptized
    February 20, 1757. p. 14

Foster, John, son of Robert and Judith. Born February 16 and Baptized
    March 17, 1771. p. 38

Foster, Joseph, son of Joel and Mary. Born June 24 and Baptized August 2,
    1772. p. 151

Foster, Joseph, son of Josiah and Caty. Born December 2, 1766 and
    Baptized February 15, 1767. p. 31

Foster, Joshua, son of Christopher and Mary. Born October 29 and Baptized
    December 1, 1776. p. 163

Foster, Joshua, son of Joshua and Elizabeth. Born August 25 and Baptized
    October 19, 1766. p. 31

Foster, Joshua, son of Joshua and Elizabeth. Born September 25 and
    Baptized October 30, 1768. p. 34

Foster, Joshua, son of Robert and Elisabeth. Born June 23 and Baptized
    July 13, 1755. p. 11

Foster, Josiah, son of John and Rose. Born December 7, 1758 and
    Baptized February 4, 1759. p. 17

Foster, Judith, daughter of Josiah and Caty. Born April 23 and Baptized
    June 3, 1764. p. 27

Foster, Judith, daughter of Mildred Bridges by R. Foster "as she sayeth".
    Born July 15 and Baptized August 6, 1769. p. 36

Foster, Judith, daughter of Robert and Elizabeth. Born February 1 and
    Baptized March 20, 1768. p. 33

Foster, Judith, daughter of Robert and Judith. Born November 26, 1775
    and Baptized January 14, 1776. p. 161

Foster, Louisa, daughter of John and Rose. Born November 2 and
    Baptized December 12, 1756. p. 13

Foster, Mary, daughter of Joshua and Elizabeth. Born February 22 and Baptized
    April 14, 1771. p. 39

Foster, Mary, daughter of Josiah and Caty. Born June 10 and Baptized
July 8, 1759. p. 18

Foster, Mary, daughter of Robert and Elizabeth. Born October 28 and
Baptized December 1, 1776. p. 163

Foster, Nanny, daughter of Robert and Judith. Born August 26 and
Baptized September 26, 1773. p. 154

Foster, Peter, son of Richard and Susannah. Born March 22 and Baptized
May 1, 1757. p. 14

Foster, Robert, son of Joshua and Sarah. Born August 2 and Baptized
August 4, 1777. p. 165

Foster, Robert, son of Robert and Elizabeth. Born November 17 and
Baptized December 11, 1757. p. 15

Foster, Rosey, daughter of John and Rose. Born May 14, 1767. p. 32

Foster, Sally, daughter of John and Rose. Born February 10 and Baptized
May 19, 1765. p. 28

Foster, Sarah, daughter of Joel and Mary. Born October 30 and Baptized
December 10, 1769. p. 36

Foster, Sarah, daughter of Robert and Elizabeth. Born May 17 and
Baptized June 20, 1762. p. 23

Foster, Susanna Ransone, daughter of Peter and Ann. Born September 3 and
Baptized October 5, 1777. p. 166

Foster, William, son of Isaac and Elizabeth. Born November 8, 1773 and
Baptized January 8, 1774. p. 155

Foster, William, son of William and Betty Jordan. Born December 29 and
Baptized December 31, 1775. p. 161

Foster, _____er, son of Joshua and Elizabeth. Baptized 1755. p. D

Foster, _____, daughter of Josiah and Caty. Baptized February 9,
1755. p. D

Fowler, Lucy Lilly, daughter of John and Ann. Born June 18 and
Baptized July 27, 1777. p. 165

G

Gale, Elizabeth, daughter of Matthew and Susannah. Born April 13 and
and Baptized June 1, 1766. p. 30

Gayle, Ambrose, son of Josiah and Mary. Born January 10 and Baptized
February 18, 1759. p. 17

Gayle, Ann, daughter of Christopher and Sarah. Born September 30 and Baptized October 17, 1756. p. 13

Gayle, Ann, daughter of George and Susannah. Born March 1, 1771. p. 39

Gayle, Ann, daughter of Josiah and Mary. Born March 10 and Baptized May 15, 1757. p. 14

Gayle, Ann, daughter of Matthew and Susannah. Born November 12, 1762 and Baptized January 30, 1763. p. 24

Gayle, Betsey, daughter of Robert and Sarah. Born ____ 2, 1773 and Baptized April 3, 1773. p. 152

Gayle, Billups, son of Matthew and Lucretia. Born July 7 and Baptized August 6, 1755. p. 11

Gayle, Caty, daughter of Thomas and Joyce. Born August 15, 1766. p. 31

Gayle, Christopher, son of Joseph and Mary. Born February 24 and Baptized April 7, 1771. p. 39

Gayle, Elly, daughter of John and Susannah. Born June 25 and Baptized August 5, 1759. p. 18

Gayle, Joanna, daughter of Matthews and Susanna. Born February 16 and Baptized April 12, 1772. p. 40

Gayle, John, son of Josiah and Mary. Born December 10, 1760 and Baptized February 1, 1761. p. 21

Gayle, John, son of Matthew and Susannah. Born December 20, 1760 and Baptized February 1, 1761. p. 21

Gayle, John Edwards, son of Thomas and Joyce. Born August 11, 1769. p. 36

Gayle, Joseph, son of Joseph and Mary. Born February 10 and Baptized March 17, 1774. p. 156

Gayle, Joseph, son of Matthias and Hannah. Born November 19, 1769 and Baptized January 21, 1770. p. 36

Gayle, Josiah, son of Robert and Sarah. Baptized April 8, 1776. p. 162

Gayle, Josiah, son of Josiah and Mary. p. A

Gayle, Joyce, daughter of John and Susanna. Born December 7, 1768. p. 34

Gayle, Leah, daughter of John and Susanna. Born January 12, 1765. p. 28

Gayle, Levin, son of John and Susannah. Born January 26 and Baptized March 13, 1763. p. 24

Gayle, Lucy, daughter of Christopher and Sarah. Born February 27 and Baptized April 2, 1758. p. 16

Gayle, Lucy, daughter of Matthew and Susanna. Born July 25 and Baptized August 5, 1775. p. 160

Gayle, Lucy Jones, daughter of Joseph and Mary. Born May 16 and Baptized June 23, 1776. p. 162

Gayle, Margaret, daughter of John and Susanna. Born April 10, 1767. p. 32

Gayle, Margaret, daughter of Matthew and Susannah. Born March 6 and Baptized April 29, 1770. p. 36

Gayle, Mary, daughter of George and Susanna. Born April 29 and Baptized June 20, 1773. p. 154

Gayle, Mary, daughter of John and Sarah. Born March 4 and Baptized May 3, 1767. p. 32

Gayle, Mary, daughter of John and Sarah. Born December 13, 1769 and Baptized January 21, 1770. p. 36

Gayle, Mary, daughter of John and Sarah. Born December 9, 1770. p. 38

Gayle, Mary, daughter of John and Susanna. Born February 14 and Baptized March 15, 1761. p. 21

Gayle, Mary, daughter of Josiah and Hannah. Born August 26, 1762. p. 23

Gayle, Mary, daughter of Matthew and Susannah. Born March 21 and Baptized April 29, 1759. p. 17

Gayle, Matthias, son of Matthias and Hannah. Born June 25 and Baptized November 29, 1767. p. 32

Gayle, Robert, son of Robert and Sarah. Born July 10 and Baptized August 20, 1769. p. 36

Gayle, Sarah, daughter of Christopher and Ann. Born December 22, 1770 and Baptized January 20, 1771. p. 38

Gayle, Sarah, daughter of John and Sarah. Born October 25 and Baptized November 27, 1768. p. 34

Gayle, Sarah, daughter of Matthew and Susanna. Born April 13 and Baptized May 15, 1767. p. 33

Gayle, Susanna, daughter of George and Susanna. Born November 12 and Baptized December 14, 1775. p. 160

Gayle, Susannah, daughter of Matthew and Susannah. Born July 7 and Baptized September 9, 1764. p. 27

Gayle, Thomas, son of Matthias and Hannah. Born February 7 and Baptized February 27, 1774. p. 156

Gayle, _____, child of George and Susanna. Born March __, 1771 and Baptized April 5, 1771. p. 39

Gibbons, Charles Blacknall, son of William and Ann. Baptized June 30, 1776. p. 162

Gibbons, Mary, daughter of William and Nancy. Born June 4 and Baptized July 5, 1772. p. 151

Gibson, _____, child of Robert and Mary. p. B

Giles, Ann, daughter of John and Ann. Born May 3 and Baptized July 25, 1773. p. 154

Glascock, Dorothy Hayes, daughter of Abraham and Elizabeth. Born August 17, and Baptized October 5, 1777. p. 166

Glascock, Elizabeth, daughter of John and Mary. Born February 3 and Baptized March 5, 1758. p. 16

Glascock, Richard, son of John and Mary. Born June 12 and Baptized July 13, 1755. p. 11

Glasgow, Elizabeth, daughter of Isaac and Ann. Born February 17 and Baptized April 8, 1773. p. 153

Glasscock, Ann, daughter of Abraham and _____. Born April 7 and Baptized May 7, 1775. p. 159

Glasscock, Mary, daughter of John and Mary. Born April 3 and Baptized June 3, 1764. p. 27

Glasscock, Richard, son of Isaac and Ann Whiting. Born November 19 and Baptized December 9, 1770. p. 38

Glasscock, Robert, son of Isaac and Ann. Born July 12 and Baptized August 4, 1775. p. 160

Glasscock, William, son of Abraham and Elizabeth. Born December 20, 1773 and Baptized February 6, 1774. p. 155

Godfrey, Eley Burd, Daughter of John and Ann. Born October 18, 1795. p.175

Godfrey, Louisa Jackson, daughter of John and Ann. Born March 19 and Baptized October 23, 1797. p. 175

Going, Ann, daughter of Joseph and Priscilla. Born June 20 and Baptized
July 4, 1762. p. 23

Green, Ann, daughter of George and Anna. Born May 7 and Baptized June 15,
1776. p. 162

Green, Ann, daughter of James and Mary. Baptized December 15, 1776. p.163

Green, Ann, daughter of John and Ann. Born March 2, and Baptized
March 12, 1773. p. 152

Green, Ann, daughter of Robert and Elizabeth. Born March 1 and Baptized
April 4, 1773. p. 153

Green, Betsy, daughter of William and Elizabeth. Born March 2 and
Baptized April 10, 1774. p. 156

Green, Caleb Hunley, son of Richard and Sally. Born June 23 and
Baptized July 17, 1774. p. 157

Green, Christopher, son of John and Ann. Born June 20 and Baptized
July 22, 1759. p. 18

Green, Elizabeth, daughter of John and Caty. Born June 11 and Baptized
June 17, 1770. p. 37

Green, Elizabeth, daughter of John and Caty. Born May 11, 1770. p. 39

Green, Elizabeth, daughter of Richard and Sarah. Born October 4 and
Baptized November 2, 1766. p. 31

Green, Elizabeth, daughter of Simon and Susanna. Born February 10 and
Baptized April 5, 1760. p. 19

Green, George, son of John and Caty. Born June 11 and Baptized July 28,
1776. p. 163

Green, George, son of Robert and Elizabeth. Baptized November 3, 1771.
p. 151

Green, James Gowing, son of John and Ann. Born February 5 and Baptized
March 25, 1764. p. 27

Green, James Hunley, son of Richard and Sarah. Born January 7 and
Baptized February 23, 1777. p. 164

Green, James and Samuel, sons of Simon and _____. Born October __,
1771 and Baptized November 1, 1771. p. 40

Green, Jenny, daughter of James and Mary. Born January 8 and Baptized
March 16, 1777. p. 164

Green, John, son of John and Ann. Born December 18, 1756 and Baptized January 23, 1757. p. 13

Green, John, son of John and Caty. Born June 16 and Baptized July 17, 1774. p. 157

Green, John, son of William and Elizabeth. Born June 25 and Baptized November 29, 1767. p. 32

Green, Joseph, son of John and Ann. Born October 16 and Baptized November 12, 1769. p. 36

Green, Martha Wescom, daughter of James and Mary. Born March 25 and Baptized April 30, 1775. p. 159

Green, Mary, daughter of William and Elizabeth. Born December 28, 1760. p. 21

Green, Mary, daughter of William and Elizabeth. Born October 17 and Baptized November 3, 1765. p. 29

Green, Nancy, daughter of William and Elizabeth. Born April 28 and Baptized May 27, 1770. p. 37

Green, Rachel, daughter of Simon and Susannah. Born September 13 and Baptized October 24, 1762. p. 24

Green, Richard, son of Richard and Sally. Born September 30 and Baptized October 27, 1771. p. 39

Green, Robert, son of George and Anna. Born January 5, 1778. p. 171

Green, Robert, son of Richard and Sally. Born March 29 and Baptized April 16, 1769. p. 35

Green, Sarah, daughter of George and Anna. Born February 25 and Baptized March 27, 1775. p. 159

Green, Simon, son of John and Ann. Born November 13 and Baptized January 10, 1762. p. 22

Green, Simon, son of Simon and Susanna. Born October 10 and Baptized November 13, 1768. p. 34

Green, William, son of John and Ann. Born May 16 and Baptized June 29, 1766. p. 30

Green, William, son of John and Caty. Born March 31 and Baptized May 10, 1772. p. 40

Green, William, son of Simon and Ann. Born January 5 and Baptized February 23, 1766. p. 30

Grigs, Susannah, daughter of George and Margaret. Born August 13 and
    Baptized September 9, 1764. p. 27

Gwyn, Daniel, son of William and Elizabeth. p. A

Gwyn, Elizabeth Toye, daughter of Humphry and Frances. Born April 25,
    and Baptized May 24, 1772. p. 151

Gwyn, Frances, daughter of Humphry and Frances. Born December 5, 1757.
    p. 15

Gwyn, Francis, daughter of William and Elizabeth. Born June 26, 1755. p.11

Gwyn, Humphry, son of Humphry and Frances. Born February 9, 1769. p. 35

Gwyn, John, son of Humphry and Frances. Born March 27, 1756. p. 12

Gwyn, Letitia Hayes, daughter of John and Dorothy. Born May 12 and
    Baptized June 9, 1774. p. 156

Gwyn, Lucy, daughter of John and Dorothy. Born November 10 and Baptized
    December 27, 1776. p. 163

Gwyn, Lucy, daughter of Humphry and Francis. Born January 10 and
    Baptized February 14, 1771. p. 38

Gwyn, Martha Peyton, daughter of Humphry and Frances. Born February 2,
    1766. p. 30

Gwyn, Mary Tabb, daughter of Humphry and Frances. Born August 22 and
    Baptized September 12, 1774. p. 157

Gwyn, Mildred, daughter of Harry and Lucy. Born March 6 and Baptized
    March 31, 1766. p. 30

Gwyn, Mildred, daughter of Humphry and Frances. Born November 23, 1759.
    p. 19

Gwyn, Thomas Peyton, son of Humphry and Frances. Born April 19, 1762.
    p. 23

H

Hackney, James Jones, son of Jacob and Ann. Born December 26, 1772 and
    Baptized January 16, 1773. p. 152

Hall, Joyce, daughter of Robert and Ann. Born February 17 and Baptized
    March 13, 1763. p. 25

Hall, Nanny, daughter of Robert and Ann. Born September 19 and Baptized
    November 14, 1756. p. 13

Hall, Robert, son of Robert and Ann. Born September 19, 1758. p. 16

Hall, Spence, son of Robert and Ann. Born November 28, 1760. p. 20

Harper, Mary, daughter of James and Elizabeth. Born March 28 and Baptized May 1, 1768. p. 33

Harper, Susanna, daughter of James and Elizabeth. Born July 17 and Baptized August 29, 1773. p. 154

Harpur, Averilla, daughter of James and Mary. Baptized September 22, 1776. p. 163

Harris, Betty James, daughter of James and Elizabeth. Born January 12 and Baptized February 18, 1770. p. 36

Harris, Elizabeth, daughter of Anthony and Dorothy. Born February 18 and Baptized February 28, 1777. p. 164

Harris, Henry, son of James and Joanna. Born December 4, 1757 and Baptized January 22, 1758. p. 15

Harris, James, son of James and Elizabeth. Born May 21 and Baptized June 18, 1775. p. 159

Harris, Jesse, son of James and Elizabeth. Born August 6 and Baptized September 7, 1766. p. 31

Harris, Joanna, daughter of Matthias and Rose. Born March 15 and Baptized April 15, 1773. p. 153

Harris, Joanna, daughter of James and Joanna. p. A

Harris, John, son of Matthias and _____. Baptized May 5, 1776. p. 162

Harris, Mary, daughter of James and Betty. Born July 4 and Baptized July 24, 1768. p. 34

Harris, Mary, daughter of Matthias and Rose. Born February 16 and Baptized March 17, 1771. p. 38

Harris, Sarah, daughter of James and Elizabeth. Born June 20 and Baptized July 19, 1772. p. 151

Harrow, Mary Moore, daughter of Thomas and Sarah Ann. Born January 1 and Baptized February 28, 1774. p. 156

Harrow, Thomas, son of Thomas and Sarah Ann. Baptized August 24, 1776. p.163

Hayes, Betty, daughter of John and Betty. Born November 17, 1773 and Baptized January 2, 1774. p. 155

Hayes, Dorothy Gwyn, daughter of John and Elizabeth. Born January 10, 1769. p. 35

Hayes, Elizabeth, daughter of Thomas and Martha. Born January 23 and
Baptized February 14, 1773. p. 152

Hayes, Hugh Elliott, son of Thomas and Martha. Born April 5 and
Baptized April 29, 1770. p. 37

Hayes, John Tabb, son of Thomas and Martha. Born June 21 and Baptized
July 24, 1768. p. 34

Hayes, John Plummer, son of John and Elizabeth. Born January 27 and
Baptized February 26, 1775. p. 158

Hayes, Mary Hardin, daughter of John and Elizabeth. Born June 22, 1767.
p. 32

Hayes, Mildred Smith, daughter of Hugh and Sarah. Born November 2, 1773
and Baptized January 27, 1774. p. 155

Hayes, Mordecai Cook, son of Thomas and Martha. Born April 17 and
Baptized May 20, 1775. p. 159

Hayes, William, son of John and Elizabeth. Born March 2 and Baptized
April 5, 1771. p. 39

Hayes, William, son of Thomas and Martha. Born May 20 and Baptized
June 12, 1757. p. 14

Hayes, William, son of Thomas and Martha. Born March 21, 1766. p. 30

Haywood, John, son of Elakin and Elizabeth. Born December 2, 1775 and
Baptized January 5, 1776. p. 161

Hensley, Polly, daughter of Joseph and Jane. Born December 6, 1774 and
Baptized March 5, 1775. p. 158

Hewel, Judy, daughter of William and Sarah. Born October 6 and Baptized
November 4, 1764. p. 28

Hewell, William Smither, son of William and Sarah. Born November 8 and
Baptized November 22, 1772. p. 152

Hill, Salley, daughter of Thomas and Ann. Born August 17 and Baptized
September 18, 1757. p. 15

Hilling, Thomas, son of William and Lucy. Born August 5 and Baptized
September 22, 1770. p. 37

Hilling, William Candy, son of William and Lucy. Born March 19 and
Baptized May 7, 1775. p. 159

Hobdy, John, son of Brookes and Mary. Born February 13 and Baptized
April 9, 1776. p. 162

Hodges, Benjamin, son of Richard and Mary. Born November 29, 1773 and Baptized February 20, 1774. p. 155

Hodges, Charles, son of Charles and Elizabeth. Born May 26, 1767. p. 32

Hodges, Mary, Sp. daughter of Ann Hodges. Born February 14 and Baptized March 29, 1777. p. 164

Hodges, Richard, son of James and Sarah. Born November 25, 1767 and Baptized January 10, 1768. p. 33

Hodges, Samuel, son of Richard and Mary. Born November 21, 1775 and Baptized February 18, 1776. p. 161

Hudgen, Aaron, son of John and Mary. Born January 15 and Baptized February 17, 1757. p. 14

Hudgen, Aaron, son of John and Ann. Born August 31 and Baptized October 30, 1768. p. 34

Hudgen, Ann, daughter of Gabriel and Sukey. Born December 20, 1763 and Baptized February 12, 1764. p. 26

Hudgen, Ann, daughter of John and Ann. Born September 29 and Baptized November 7, 1773. p. 155

Hudgen, Anthony, son of William and Joanna. Born July 24 and Baptized August 21, 1757. p. 15

Hudgen, Archibald, son of George and Dorothy. Born September 18 and Baptized October 19, 1766. p. 31

Hudgen, Averilla, daughter of George and Dorothy. Born June 16 and Baptized July 10, 1768. p. 34

Hudgen, Averillah, daughter of George and Hillegin. Born July 20, 1755. p. 11

Hudgen, Basshe (Bathsheba), daughter of James and Ann. Born December 20, 1763 and Baptized February 12, 1764. p. 26

Hudgen, Caty, daughter of Lewis and Joyce. Born July 18 and Baptized August 24, 1766. p. 31

Hudgen, Christopher, bastard son of Suky Hudgen. Born November 8 and Baptized December 9, 1770. p. 38

Hudgen, Dolly, daughter of William and Sarah. Born February 16 and Baptized April 8, 1764. p. 27

Hudgen, Edwards, son of William and Elizabeth. Born March 3 and Baptized March 27, 1763. p. 25

Hudgen, Elizabeth, daughter of Aaron and Mary. Born June 24 and Baptized
    August 5, 1759. p. 18

Hudgen, Elizabeth, daughter of John and Ann. Born September 16 and
    Baptized November 2, 1766. p. 31

Hudgen, Elizabeth, daughter of John and Ann. Born February 23 and
    Baptized March 17, 1771. p. 38

Hudgen, Emmanuel, son of Aaron and Mary. Born March 13 and Baptized
    March 28, 1762. p. 22

Hudgen, Fanny, daughter of William and Frances. Born February 22 and
    Baptized April 12, 1772. p. 40

Hudgen, George, son of Gabriel and Lucretia. Born September 29 and
    Baptized November 2, 1766. p. 31

Hudgen, Holder, son of John and Sarah. Born April 14 and Baptized
    June 18, 1771. p. 39

Hudgen, Hugh, son of George and Dorothy. Born January 29 and Baptized
    February 28, 1773. p. 152

Hudgen, Humphry, son of Humphry and Joanna. Born August 7, 1757. p. 15

Hudg(en), Humphry, son of John and Ann. Born September 26, ____. p. C

Hudgen, Humphry, son of William and Dorothy. Born August 11, 1765. p.29

Hudgen, Isaac, son of Lewis and Joyce. Born September 5 and Baptized
    October 22, 1775. p. 160

Hudgen, Isaac, son of William and Joana. Born March 17 and Baptized
    April 26, 1772. p. 40

Hudgen, James, son of Aaron and Joann. Born May 17 and Baptized June 7,
    1761. p. 21

Hudgen, James, son of Gabriel and Suky. Born October 15 and Baptized
    December 9, 1770. p. 38

Hudgen, James, son of James and Rebecca. Born October 22 and Baptized
    November 25, 1759. p. 19

Hudgen, James, son of William and Elizabeth. Born November 4 and
    Baptized December 27, 1767. p. 33

Hudgen, Jesse, son of Perrin and Sarah. Born May 26 and Baptized
    June 18, 1775. p. 159

Hudgen, Joanna, daughter of Moses and Mildred. Born November 7, 1768. p.34

Hudgen, Joannah, daughter of John and Ann. Born June 28 and Baptized July 13, 1766. p. 30

Hudgen, John, son of Alban and Elizabeth. Born August 11 and Baptized October 9, 1763. p. 26

Hudgen, John, son of Gabriel and Lucretia. Born December 31, 1756 and Baptized March 1, 1757. p. 13

Hudgen, John, son of Humphry and Johannah. Born October 8 and Baptized November 21, 1762. p. 24

Hudgen, John, son of James and Ann. Born April 20 and Baptized May 23, 1762. p. 23

Hudgen, John, son of John and Ann. Born September 18 and Baptized October 27, 1771. p. 39

Hudgen, John, son of Lewis and Elizabeth. Born March 6, 1760. p. 19

Hudgen, John, son of Lewis and Joyce. Born September 15, 1770. p. 37

Hudgen, John, son of William and Dorothy. Born January 19 and Baptized February 18, 1770. p. 36

Hudgen, John, son of William and Frances. Born May 19 and Baptized June 20, 1762. p. 23

Hudgen, John, son of William and Sarah. Born September 24, ____. p. C

Hudgen, Joshua, son of John and Ann. Born June 25 and Baptized August 6, 1769. p. 35

Hudgen, Joshua Degge, son of James and Rebecca. Born May 30 and Baptized June 25, 1758. p. 16

Hudgen, Joyce, daughter of Lewis and Joyce. Born March 9 and Baptized May 9, 1773. p. 153

Hudgen, Judith, daughter of James and Ann. Born December 10, 1765 and Baptized February 23, 1766. p. 29

Hudgen, Kemp, a bastard child of Elizabeth Hudgen. Born September 20 and Baptized November 14, 1756. p. 13

Hudgen, Lewis, son of William and Sarah. Born August 20 and Baptized September 21, 1766. p. 31

Hudgen, Mary, daughter of Alban and Elizabeth. Born March 31 and Baptized April 26, 1772. p. 40

Hudgen, Mary, daughter of James and Ann. Born May 1 and Baptized June 26, 1768. p. 33

Hudgen, Mary, daughter of William and Sarah. Born November 9, 1759. p. 19

Hudgen, Mildred, daughter of John and Mary. Born June 3, 1764. p. 27

Hudgen, Milley, daughter of Lewis and Joyce. Born May 1 and Baptized June 12, 1768. p. 33

Hudgen, Milley, daughter of William and Joannah. Born June 10 and Baptized July 8, 1759. p. 18

Hudgen, Milly, daughter of William and Sarah. Born May 30 and Baptized June 25, 1769. p. 35

Hudgen, Molly, daughter of Jane Summers by Joshua Hudgen. Born April 1 and Baptized April 29, 1770. p. 37

Hudgen, Moses, son of Ambrose and Ann. Born October 11 and Baptized November 13, 1757. p. 15

Hudgen, Moses, son of Moses and Mary. Born June 28 and Baptized July 31, 1763. p. 25

Hudgen, Nancy, daughter of Joshua and Jenny. Born August 25 and Baptized September 26, 1773. p. 154

Hudgen, Nancy, daughter of Moses and Elizabeth. Born October 17 and Baptized December 10, 1769. p. 36

Hudgen, Robert, son of Moses and Mildred. Born November 12 and Baptized November 24, 1771. p. 40

Hudgen, Robert, son of William and Sarah. Born March 9 and Baptized April 12, 1772. p. 40

Hudgen, Sarah, daughter of Gabriel and Sukey. Born September 4 and Baptized October 12, 1758. p. 16

Hudgen, Sarah, daughter of Moses and Mary. Born June 13, 1759. p. 18

Hudgen, Sarah, daughter of William and Sarah. Born November 11 and Baptized December 12, 1756. p. 13

Hudgen, Sarah, daughter of William and Joannah. Born July 26 and Baptized August 24, 1776. p. 31

Hudgen, Sukey, daughter of Gabriel and Sukey. Born December 9, 1760 and Baptized February 15, 1761. p. 21

Hudgen, Susanna Sanford, daughter of William and Frances. Born March __, and Baptized March 22, 1761. p. 21

Hudgen, William, son of Lewis and Elizabeth. Born December 12, 1758. p.17

Hudgen, William, son of William and Dorothy. Born June 17 and Baptized
November 15, 1767. p. 32

Hudgen, William, son of William and Frances. Born December 17, 1767. p.33

Hudgen, William, son of William and Joanna. Born November 4, 1761 and
Baptized January 10, 1762. p. 22

Hudgen, William, son of William and Sarah. Born December 21, 1761 and
Baptized January 31, 1762. p. 22

Hudgen, William Holder, son of Robert and Annah. Born January 14 and
Baptized February 12, 1764. p. 26

Hudgen, _____, child of _____ and Joannah. p. D

Hudgin, Ann and Elizabeth, twins of Alban and Elizabeth. Born August 30
and Baptized September 10, 1775. p. 160

Hudgin, Ann Jarvis, daughter of James and Ann. Born December 11, 1773 and
Baptized February 19, 1774. p. 155

Hudgin, Ann Willis, daughter of Holder and Mary. Born _____, 1773 and
Baptized February 19, 1774. p. 155

Hudgin, Anthony, son of Anthony and Salley. Born December 28, 1781. p. 171

Hudgin, Anthony, son of Lewis and Joyce. Born September 14 and Baptized
October 19, 1777. p. 166

Hudgin, Archibald and Joanna, twins, son and daughter of William Hudgin,
deceased, and Dorothy. Born December 22 and Baptized December 31,
1772. p. 152

Hudgin, Betty, daughter of Kemp and Joice. Born August __, 1780. p. 171

Hudgin, Beverley, son of John and Mary. Baptized October 26, 1777. p. 166

Hudgin, Diggs, son of Anthony and Salley. Born March 4, 1786. p. 173

Hudgin, Dorothy, daughter of Gabriel and Suky. Baptized February 27, 1774.
p. 155

Hudgin, Elizabeth, daughter of William and Elizabeth. Born June 4 and
Baptized July 8, 1770. p. 37

Hudgin, Frances, daughter of Moses and Elizabeth. Born October 18 and
Baptized November 22, 1772. p. 152

Hudgin, Humphrey, son of John and Amelia. Born December 8, 1794. p. 174

Hudgin, Hunley, son of Anthony and Sally. Born September 11, 1780. p. 171

Hudgin, Isaac, son of Anthony and Salley. Born April 4, 1782. p. 171

Hudgin, Iveson, son of John and Mary. Born November 7 and Baptized December 17, 1775. p. 161

Hudgin, James, son of John and Ann. Born August 30, 1798. p. 176

Hudgin, John Wilson, bastard son of Catharine Hudgin. Born January 12, 1796. p. 175

Hudgin, John, son of John and Catharine. Born April 13, 1816. p. 178

Hudgin, John, son of John and Mary. Born March 6 and Baptized May 25, 1790. p. 173

Hudgin, John, son of John and Sarah. Born September 8 and Baptized November 2, 1777. p. 166

Hudgin, John, son of William and Maryan. Born August 30, 1789. p. 173

Hudgin, Lucyna, daughter of John and Catharine. Born May 17, 1819. p. 178

Hudgin, Mary, daughter of Anthony and Salley. Born August 10, 1793. p. 174

Hudgin, Nancy, Sp. daughter of Suky Hudgin. Born March 27 and and Baptized April 14, 1774. p. 156

Hudgin, Peter, son of Anthony and Salley. Born October 19, 1787. p.172

Hudgin, Polley, daughter of John and Ann. Born March 22, 1796. p. 175

Hudgin, Polly, daughter of John and Mary. Born May 27, 1788. p. 173

Hudgin, Robert, son of John and Ann. Born May 2, 1801. p. 176

Hudgin, Rose, daughter of Humphry and Louisa. Baptized October 20, 1776. p. 163

Hudgin, Sally, daughter of Hugh and _____. Baptized October 30, 1774. p. 157

Hudgin, Sarah, daughter of Anthony and Salley. Born March 10, 1791. p.173

Hudgin, Sarah, daughter of William and Frances. Born August 16 and Baptized September 8, 1776. p. 163

Hudgin, Thomas, son of John and Ann. Baptized March 24, 1776. p. 162

Hudgin, Wescom, son of Robert and Elizabeth. Born December 31, 1773 and Baptized February 12, 1774. p. 155

Hudgin, William, son of Anthony and Salley. Born January 23, 1779. p. 171

Hudgin, William, son of John and Sarah. Born June __, 1774 and Baptized July 31, 1774. p. 157

Hudgin, William, son of Moses and Elizabeth. Born July 25 and Baptized August 18, 1776. p. 163

Hudgin, _____, son of John and Catharine. Born March 20, 1812. p. 177

Hudgins, Betsy, daughter of John and Ann. Born August 23, 1803. p. 176

Hudgins, Betsy Soper, daughter of John and Ann. Born October 9, 1797. p.175

Hudgins, Elizabeth, daughter of William and Elizabeth. Born June 4 and Baptized June 14, 1770. p. 37

Hudgins, Gideon Washington, son of John and Ann. Born March 20, 1799. p.176

Hudgins, John Foster, son of John and Amelia. Born January 26, 1787. p.172

Hudgins, Mary Degge, daughter of John and Amelia. Born March 29, 1783. p.171

Hudgins, Rosanna, daughter of John and Amelia. Born January 6, 1791. p. 173

Huell, Milly, daughter of William and Sarah. Born January __, 1763 and Baptized April 10, 1763. p. 24

Hugate, Alice, daughter of James and Ann. Born March 30 and Baptized May 15, 1757. p. 14

Hugget, Dolly, daughter of James and Elizabeth. Born March 23 and Baptized May 4, 1766. p. 30

Hughes, Edward, son of Edward and Elizabeth. Born August 13, 1760. p. 20

Hughes, Elizabeth, daughter of Edward and Elizabeth. Born August 18, 1762. p. 23

Hughes, Elizabeth Jones, daughter of Gabriel and Ann. Born September 7 and Baptized November 13, 1768. p. 34

Hughes, Francis, son of Gabriel and Ann. Born January 11, 1761. p. 21

Hughes, Harriet, daughter of Gabriel and Ann. Born April 3 and Baptized April 3, 1771. p. 39

Hughes, Hugh, son of Gabriel and Ann. Baptized April 28, 1776. p. 162

Hughes, John, son of Edward and Elizabeth. Baptized October 14, 1774. p. 157

Hughes, Lux, son of Edward and Elizabeth. Born February 1, 1765. p. 28

Hughes, Richard, son of Edward and Elizabeth. Born January 11 and
 Baptized January 31, 1771. p. 38

Hughes, Robert, son of Gabriel and Ann. Born November 20 and
 Baptized December 1, 1766. p. 31

Hughes, Susanna Throckmorton, daughter of Gabriel and Ann. Born
 March 21 and Baptized May 6, 1773. p. 153

Hughes, Susannah, daughter of Edward and Elizabeth. Born December 16,
 1766 and Baptized February 12, 1767. p. 31

Hughes, Thomas, son of Edward and Elizabeth. Born June 27, 1758. p.16

Hughes, Thomas, son of Gabriel and Ann. Born March 6, 1758. p. 16

Hughes, William, son of Edward and Elizabeth. Born February 6,1769. p.35

Hundley, Ann, daughter of John and Mary. Born May 29 and Baptized
 June 27, 1756. p. 12

Hundley, Elisabeth, daughter of John and Elisabeth. Born January 27
 and Baptized March 23, 1777. p. 164

Hundley, Elisabeth, daughter of Matthew and Lettitia. Born July 22 and
 Baptized August 2, 1755. p. 11

Hundley, (Ja)mes, son of Thomas and Sarah. Born December 21, 1755. p.11

Hundley, Judith, daughter of James and Mary. Born December __, 1765
 and Baptized January 12, 1766. p. 29

Hundley, Nanny, daughter of James and Mary. Born April 3 and Baptized
 June 25, 1769. p. 35

Hundley, Richard, son of Matthew and Lettitia. Born November 19 and
 Baptized December 9, 1759. p. 19

Hundley, Sarah, daughter of James and Mary. Born February __, 1767. p.31

Hundley, _____, son of Henry and Joyce. Baptized 1755. p. D

Hunley, Ann, daughter of Henry and Joyce. Born May 31 and Baptized
 June 24, 1759. p. 18

Hunley, Anthony, son of Nehemiah and Ann. Born November 24, 1787. p.172

Hunley, Anthony and Matthias, sons of Thomas and Mary. Born August 28,
 and Baptized August 29, 1771. p. 39

Hunley, Anthony, son of Wilkinson and Rose. Born April 23 and Baptized
 May 28, 1758. p. 16

Hunley, Dorothy, daughter of Ransone and Elizabeth. Born November __,
 1760 and Baptized February 1, 1761. p. 20

Hunley, Elizabeth, daughter of John and Mary. Born January 3 and
  Baptized February 3, 1760. p. 19

Hunley, Frankey, daughter of Henry and Joyce. Born June 3 and Baptized
  July 18, 1762. p. 23

Hunley, George, son of James and Mary. Born August 6 and Baptized
  September 10, 1774. p. 157

Hunley, Humphry, son of Ransone and Elizabeth. Born August 6 and Baptized
  October 1, 1763. p. 26

Hunley, James, son of Robert and Joyce. Born April 18 and Baptized May 31,
  1775. p. 159

Hunley, James Harris, son of John and Parthenia. Born March 24 and
  Baptized May 3, 1774. p. 156

Hunley, Jeriah, daughter of Caleb and Jane. Born April 6, 1759. p. 17

Hunley, John, son of Henry and Mary. Baptized April 3, 1773. p. 152

Hunley, John, son of Matthias and Sary. Baptized February 3, 1778. p. 171

Hunley, John, son of Ransone and Elizabeth. Born May 1 and Baptized
  June 1, 1766. p. 30

Hunley, John, son of Richard and Sarah. Baptized August 8, 1777. p. 165

Hunley, John Biggs, son of James and Mary. Born January 26 and Baptized
  April 14, 1771. p. 39

Hunley, Joyce, daughter of Ransone and Elizabeth. Born _____, 1771 and
  Baptized December 13, 1771. p. 40

Hunley, Joyce Smith, daughter of William and Elizabeth. Born January 24,
  1797. p. 175

Hunley, Lettitia, daughter of Matthew and Lettitia. Born July 30 and
  Baptized August 25, 1765. p. 29

Hunley, Letitia, daughter of Thomas and Mary. Born August 15 and Baptized
  September 24, 1775. p. 160

Hunley, Mary, daughter of Henry and Joyce. Born August 4 and Baptized
  October 2, 1757. p. 15

Hunley, Mary, daughter of William and Elizabeth. Born February 27, 1793.
  p. 174

Hunley, Matthew, son of William and Elisabeth. Born September 28 and
  Baptized November 2, 1777. p. 166

Hunley, Matthew, son of Matthew and Lettitia. Born September 12 and
Baptized October 24, 1762. p. 24

Hunley, Nancy, daughter of Wilkinson and Rose. Born December 30, 1764.
p. 28

Hunley, Nanny, daughter of Thomas and Mary. Born August 26, 1761. p. 22

Hunley, Nehemiah, son of Henry and Joyce. Born February 11 and Baptized
March 9, 1766. p. 30

Hunley, Philip, son of Matthew and Letitia. Born August 28 and Baptized
October 2, 1757. p. 15

Hunley, Richard, son of Robert and Sarah. Born October 12 and Baptized
November 13, 1757. p. 15

Hunley, Robert, son of Caleb and Elizabeth. Born August 2 and Baptized
August 10, 1775. p. 160

Hunley, Sarah, daughter of John and Mary. Born January 25 and Baptized
February 19, 1758. p. 16

Hunley, Thomas, son of Ambrose and Mary. Born August 20 and Baptized
September 26, 1762. p. 23

Hunley, Thomas, a bastard son of Susannah Hunley. Born September __, 1764
and Baptized October 21, 1764. p. 28

Hunley, William, son of John and Parthenia. Born November 30 and
Baptized December 15, 1766. p. 31

Hunley, William, son of William and Elizabeth. Born November 24, 1783. p.
p. 171

Hunley, _____, daughter of Richard and Ann. p. B

Hunly, Lettitia, daughter of William and Elizabeth. Born March 8, 1800.
p. 176

Hurst, Betsy, daughter of Richard and Mildred. Born January 24 and
Baptized February 14, 1773. p. 152

Hurst, Frances, daughter of Richard and Mildred. Born May 5, 1769. p.35

Hurst, Jesse, son of Richard and Mildred. Born October 23, 1766. p. 31

Hurst, John, son of John and Elizabeth. Born July 2 and Baptized
August 15, 1762. p. 23

Hurst, John, son of Richard and Mildred. Born July 17 and Baptized
August 19, 1759. p. 18

Hurst, Richard, son of John and Elizabeth. Born February 10, 1760. p. 19

Hurst, Richard, son of Richard and Mildred. Born March 3, 1762. p. 22

Hurst, Sarah, daughter of John and Elizabeth. Born November 20, 1768 and Baptized January 22, 1769. p. 34

Hurst, Sarah, daughter of Richard and Mildred. Born March 26 and Baptized April 6, 1775. p. 159

Hurst, William, son of John and Elizabeth. Born May 22 and Baptized June 29, 1766. p. 30

Hurst, William, son of Richard and Mildred. Born April 28 and Baptized June 3, 1764. p. 27

I

Iveson, Fanny, daughter of Abraham and Mary. Born March 22 and Baptized May 28, 1777. p. 165

J

Jackman, William, son of John and Mary. Born March 1 and Baptized April 13, 1777. p. 164

Jackson, John, son of John and _____. Born March 15 and Baptized April 4, 1773. p. 153

Jackson, William, son of George and Mary. Born July 19 and Baptized September 9, 1764. p. 27

Jackson, William, son of John and Anna. Born November 11, 1770. p. 38

Jacson, John, son of George and Mary. Born February 20, 1761. p. 21

Jacson, Judith, daughter of George and Mary. Born December 14, 1758 and Baptized January 21, 1759. p. 17

James, Catherine, daughter of Matthias and Elizabeth. Born February 26 and Baptized May 1, 1768. p. 33

James, Cary, son of Thomas and Betsy. Born September 27, 1795. p. 175

James, Cyrum Cooper, daughter of Cyrus B. and Mary. Born January 22, 1812. p. 177

James, Cyrus Basey, son of Thomas and Betsy. Born August 7, 1786. p. 172

James, Edward, son of Mathias and Elizabeth. Born May 4 and Baptized June 29, 1766. p. 30

James, Elizabeth, daughter of Matthias and Elizabeth. Born September 17 and Baptized October 16, 1772. p. 151

James, Elizabeth Hunley, daughter of Thomas and Betsey. Born January 2, 1788. p. 172

James, Frances, daughter of Thomas and Betsy. Born November 8, 1784. p. 172

James, Harriot Smith, daughter of Thomas and Betty. Born January 25, 1805. p. 176

James, Hilligan Degge, daughter of Thomas and Betsy. Born March 26, 1802. p. 176

James, John, son of Walter and Sarah. Born February 21 and Baptized April 1, 1770. p. 36

James, Martha Washington, daughter of Thomas and Betsy. Born March 8, 1800. p. 176

James, Matthias, son of Matthias and Elizabeth. Born November 2 and Baptized December 4, 1774. p. 157

James, Matthias, son of Walter and Sarah. Born April 4 and Baptized May 10, 1772. p. 40

James, Miriam Marshall, daughter of Thomas and Betsy. Born February 8, 1798. p. 176

James, Paulina, daughter of Thomas and Betsy. Born October 27, 1790 and Baptized February 27, 1791. p. 173

James, Richard, son of Walter and Sarah. Born May 18 and Baptized June 15, 1777. p. 165

James, Susanna, daughter of Matthias and Elizabeth. Born February 20 and Baptized March 18, 1770. p. 36

James, Thomas, son of Matthias and Elisabeth. Born February 24 and Baptized March 23, 1777. p. 164

James, Thomas Degge Davis, son of Thomas and Betsey James. Born August 7, 1792. p. 174

James, Thomas Edward, son of Cyrus B. and Mary. Born _____, 1817. p. 178

James, Walter, son of Walter and Sarah. Born October 2 and Baptized November 6, 1774. p. 157

James, William Leven, son of Thomas and Betsy. Born January 20, 1808. p. 177

James, William, son of Walter and Sarah.   Born January 15 and Baptized
    February 21, 1768. p. 33

James, _____, son of Cyrus and Mary. Born October ____, 1813. p. 177

Jarret, George, son of John and _____. Baptized July 28, 1776. p.163

Jarret, William, son of John and Ann. Born August 17 and Baptized
    September 21, 1766. p. 31

Jarrett, Annah, daughter of Thomas and Elizabeth. Born May 20 and Baptized
    June 19, 1763. p. 25

Jarrett, Betty, daughter of Thomas and Elizabeth. Born May 30, 1759. p. 18

Jarvis, Betty, daughter of William and Lucy.   p. A

Jarvis, Edward, son of Francis and Elizabeth. Born October 18 and Baptized
    December 4, 1763. p. 26

Jervis, Ann, daughter of James and Lucy. Born March 11 and Baptized April 23,
    1775. p. 159

Jervis, Bannister, son of William and Lucy. Born August 31 and Baptized
    October 21, 1764. p. 27

Jervis, Betty, daughter of Francis and Ann. Born December 24, 1770 and
    Baptized February 2, 1771. p. 38

Jervis, Elisabeth, daughter of James and Lucy. Born November 15 and Baptized
    December 7, 1777. p. 166

Jervis, Elizabeth, daughter of John and Sally. Born July 27 and Baptized
    August 27, 1775. p. 160

Jervis, Elizabeth, daughter of John and Mary. Born March __, 1776 and
    Baptized March 23, 1776. p. 162

Jervis, Francis, son of Francis and Elizabeth. Born August 28, ____. p. C

Jervis, Francis, son of William and Lucy. Born July 31 and Baptized
    September 20, 1767. p. 32

Jervis, Garvin, son of William and Lucy. Born June 22 and Baptized July 18,
    1773. p. 154

Jervis, John, son of Francis and Ann. Born April 17 and Baptized May 13,
    1770. p. 37

Jervis, John, son of Francis and Ann. Born March 22 and Baptized April 24,
    1773. p. 153

Jervis, John, son of Francis and Elizabeth. Born July 18 and Baptized
    September 5, 1756. p. 12

Jervis, John Dixon, son of Lindsey and Elizabeth. Born August 21 and
	September 3, 1773. p. 154

Jervis, Lucy, daughter of William and Lucy. Born November 10, 1761 and
	Baptized January 10, 1762. p. 22

Jervis, Mary, daughter of John and Sarah. Born January 7, and Baptized
	February 5, 1777. p. 164

Jervis, Mary, daughter of William and Lucy. Born April 20 and Baptized
	June 12, 1757. p. 14

Jervis, Patty Read, daughter of Francis and Ann. Born August 20 and
	Baptized September 25, 1774. p. 157

Jervis, Thomas, son of Thomas and Sarah. Born May 7 and Baptized
	June 27, 1756. p. 12

Jervis, Thomas William, son of Francis and Elizabeth. Born March 1 and
	Baptized April 29, 1759. p. 17

Jervis, William, son of Francis and Ann. Baptized August 4, 1776. p. 163

Jervis, William, son of William and Lucy. Born May 9 and Baptized
	June 24, 1759. p. 18

Johnson, Elizabeth, daughter of John and Judith. Born September 5,
	1757. p. 15

Johnson, Frankey, daughter of John and Judith. Born February 17, 1761. p. 21

Johnson, Jane, daughter of Hugh and Mary. Born September 21 and Baptized
	October 23, 1774. p. 157

Johnson, Patty, daughter of John and Judith. Born January 12, 1761. p. 21

Johnson, Polly Flipping, daughter of John and Judith. Baptized
	June 16, 1771. p. 151

Jones, Ann, daughter of Thomas and Ann. Born August 24 and Baptized
	September 20, 1767. p. 32

Jones, Charles, son of Charles and Letititia. Born December 24, 1787.
	p. 172

Jones, Dorothy Cary, daughter of James and Dorothy. Baptized January 17,
	1776. p. 161

Jones, Edward, son of Thomas and Ann. Baptized February 24, 1777. p.164

Jones, Elizabeth Callis, daughter of Thomas and Ann. Born November 24,
	and Baptized December 9, 1770. p. 38

Jones, George W., son of Charles and Lettitia. Born December 26, 1791 and departed July 15, 1793. p. 173

Jones, James R., son of Charles and Lettitia. Born April 13, 1786. p. 172

Jones, James W., son of James and Frances. Born June 2, 1788. p. 173

Jones, Joyce, daughter of Thomas and Ann. Born May 14 and Baptized June 19, 1763. p. 25

Jones, Martha H., daughter of Charles and Letitia. Born November 16, 1789. p. 173

Jones, Robert, son of Thomas and Ann. Born September 22 and Baptized October 23, 1774. p. 157

Jones, Sally, daughter of Thomas and Ann. Born July 17, 1765. p. 29

Jones, Thomas, son of Thomas and Ann. Born January 22 and Baptized February 13, 1773. p. 152

K

Keeble, Lucy, daughter of Walter and Elizabeth. Born January 26, 1759. p. 17

Kees, Lucy, daughter of Howard and Ann. Born November 1, 1762 and Baptized March 13, 1763. p. 24

Kees, Sally, daughter of Edward and Catherine. Born July 18, 1780. p. 171

Kees, _____, daughter of John and Damaris. Born May 5 and Baptized June 1, 1755. p. 11

Kemp, Gregory, son of William and Elizabeth. Born October 17 and Baptized December 3, 1774. p. 157

Keys, Ann, daughter of Robert and Sarah. Born October 29, 1759 and Baptized November 25, 1759. p. 19

Keys, Betty, daughter of Robert and Sarah. Born January 20 and Baptized March 10, 1765. p. 28

Keys, Hillegan, daughter of Robert and Sarah. Born February 23 and Baptized March 20, 1768. p. 33

Keys, John, son of Edward and Caty. Born March 7 and Baptized March 23, 1776. p. 162

Keys, John, son of Howard and Ann. Born May 16 and Baptized May 27, 1759. p. 18

Keys, Mary, daughter of Howard and Ann. Born July 17 and Baptized August 22, 1756. p. 12

Keys, Sally, daughter of Howard and Ann. Born May 15 and Baptized
    October 4, 1767. p. 32

Keys, (Sa)lley, daughter of Robert and Sarah. Born December 23, 1755. p.11

King, Alexander, son of Joseph and Nanny. Born June 23, 1763. p. 25

King, James, son of John and Mary. Born January 17 and Baptized March 16,
    1777. p. 164

King, James, son of Joseph and Ann. Baptized June 31, 1771. p. 151

King, John, son of John and Mary. Born November 4 and Baptized
    December 6, 1774. p. 158

King, Joseph, son of Thomas and Elizabeth. Baptized October 4, 1772. p.151

King, Mary Ann, daughter of Thomas and Elizabeth. Born September 27 and
    Baptized November 13, 1774. p. 157

King, Nanny, daughter of Joseph and Nanny. Born July 31, 1759. p. 18

King, Snelling, son of Joseph and Nanny. Born January 5, 1757. p. 14

King, Thomas, son of Thomas and Elizabeth. Born December __, 1770 and
    Baptized February 24, 1771. p. 38

Kinnun, Elizabeth, daughter of Aristarcus and _____. Born August 3 and
    Baptized September 18, 1757. p.15

Knigh(t), Joseph, son of Henry and Elizabeth. Born January 22 and Baptized
    February 28, 1762. p. 22

Knight, Betsy, daughter of John and Elizabeth. Born April 3 and
    Baptized May 10, 1772. p. 40

Knight, Gabriel, son of Henry and Elizabeth. Born April 7 and Baptized
    July 23, 1769. p. 35

Knight, Henry, son of Henry and Elizabeth. Born June 5 and Baptized
    July 19, 1758. p. 16

Knight, Humphry, son of Henry and Elizabeth. Born January 8 and Baptized
    February 3, 1760. p. 19

Knight, John, son of Henry and Elizabeth. Born January 6 and Baptized
    March 13, 1774. p. 156

Knight, Mary, daughter of Henry and Elizabeth. Born January 18 and
    Baptized February 23, 1766. p. 30

Knight, Richard, son of Henry and Elizabeth. Born July 13 and Baptized
    September 19, 1756. p. 12

Knight, Sarah, daughter of Henry and Elizabeth. Born December 14, 1776 and Baptized March 9, 1777. p. 164

Knightman, Samuel Thompson, son of Henry and Elizabeth. Born January 14 and Baptized February 25, 1764. p. 26

L

Lane, Susanna Street, a bastard daughter of Mary Lane. Born March 20 and Baptized April 26, 1772. p. 40

Layton, Reuben, son of Reuben and Elizabeth Layton. Born August 26 and Baptized October 3, 1773. p. 154

Lewis, Christopher, son of Thomas and Mary. Born July 17 and Baptized July 30, 1775. p. 160

Lewis, Elisabeth, daughter of John and Elisabeth. Born December 27, 1775 and Baptized January 6, 1776. p. 161

Lewis, Elizabeth, daughter of Christopher and Caty. Born September 13, 1769. p. 36

Lewis, George, son of Robert and Elizabeth. Born May 11 and Baptized June 16, 1776. p. 162

Lewis, Johannah, daughter of John and Lucretia. Born July 1, ____. p. C

Lewis, John, son of Robert and Elizabeth. Born November 22, 1773 and Baptized January 16, 1774. p. 155

Lewis, Lucretia, daughter of Christopher and Caty. Born May 23 and Baptized June 18, 1775. p. 159

Lewis, Mary, daughter of Robert and Elizabeth. Born December __, 1770 and Baptized February 3, 1771. p. 38

Lewis, Nancy, daughter of John and Elizabeth. Born October 28 and Baptized November 27, 1773. p. 155

Lewis, Nanny, daughter of Thomas and Elizabeth. Born December 21, 1763 and Baptized January 15, 1764. p. 26

Lewis, Thomas, son of John and Elisabeth. Born May 16 and Baptized June 29, 1777. p. 165

Lewis, _____, son of John and Lucretia. p. B

Lichfield, Hezekiah, son of Francis and Elizabeth. Born September 21 and Baptized October 1, 1758. p. 17

Lichfield, John, son of Francis and Elizabeth. Born September 25, 1760. p. 20

Lilly, Ann, daughter of William and Lucy. Born January 4 and Baptized
     February 5, 1758. p. 16

Lilly, John, son of William and Lucy. Born August 12, 1761. p. 22

Lilly, Richard, son of William and Lucy. Born February 14 and Baptized
     March 29, 1772. p. 40

Lilly, Thomas, son of William and Lucy. Born February 26, 1765. p. 28

Lilly, William Armistead, son of William and Lucy. Born April __, 1767.
     p. 32

Lilly, _____y, daughter of William and Lucy. Born December 19, 1755. p.11

Little, Elizabeth, daughter of John and Susanna. Born June 5 and
     Baptized November 29, 1767. p. 32

Little, Caty, daughter of John and Susanna. Born October 24, 1769. p.36

Little, Mary, daughter of John and Susanna. Born October 16 and
     Baptized December 6, 1772. p. 152

Little, Susanna, daughter of John and Susanna. Born December 29, 1775
     and Baptized March 10, 1776. p. 161

Longest, Caleb, son of Joshua and Elizabeth. Born May 1 and Baptized
     June 12, 1757. p. 14

Longest, Dorothy, daughter of Richard and Ann. Born May 15 and Baptized
     July 1, 1764. p. 27

Longest, Frankey, daughter of Richard and Ann. Born February 14, 1758
     p. 16

Longest, James, son of Joshua and Elizabeth. Born January 28 and
     Baptized March 19, 1769. p. 35

Longest, John Jones, son of Thomas and Ann. Born February 7 and Baptized
     March 6, 1774. p. 156

Longest, Joshua, son of Joshua and Elizabeth. Born May 21 and Baptized
     July 20, 1760. p. 20

Longest, Joshua Floyd, son of Joshua and Elizabeth. Born October 27 and
     Baptized December 16, 1764. p. 28

Longest, Mildred, daughter of Joshua and Mildred. Born February 20, 1756.
     p. 12

Longest, Nancy, daughter of Richard and Ann. Born August 30 and Baptized
     October 17, 1756. p. 12

Longest, Richard, son of Richard and Ann. Born July 3, 1767. p. 32

Longest, Richard, son of William and Ann. Born August 19, 1757. p. 15

Longest, Robert Ross, son of Richard and Ann. Born November 14, 1761. p.22

Longest, Thomas, son of Thomas and Ann. Born June 8 and Baptized July 9, 1775. p. 160

Longest, _____, daughter of Richard and Ann. p. B

Lovel, Mary, daughter of Richard and Sarah. Born April 10, 1758. p. 16

Lucas, Mary Blacknall, daughter of William and Mary. Born June 24 and Baptized July 31, 1774. p. 157

Lunsford, Hiram L., son of Thomas L. and Sarah L. Born February 13, 1803. p.17

Lyle, James, son of John and Mary. Born March 28 and Baptized March 28, 1777. p. 164

Mc

McCoy, Daniel, son of Charles and Joanna. Born February 25 and Baptized May 8, 1774. p. 156

McCoy, George, son of Charles and Joanna. Born October 13 and Baptized December 11, 1768. p. 34

McCoy, Joseph, son of Charles and Joannah. Born October 10 and Baptized November 24, 1771. p. 40

Macdougal, James, son of Daniel and Elisabeth. Born April 10 and Baptized May 11, 1777. p. 165

McDougal, John, son of Daniel and Elizabeth. Born October 8 and Baptized October 30, 1774. p. 157

M

Machen, Averilla, daughter of William and Sârah. Born April 19 and Baptized May 10, 1772. p. 151

Machen, Elizabeth, daughter of Robert and Ann. Born January 9 and Baptized February 14, 1762. p. 22

Machen, John, son of John and Mary. Born December 5, 1780. p. 171

Machen, John, son of Robert and Ann. Born January 26, 1767. p. 31

Machen, John, son of Samuel and Nanny. Born February 8 and Baptized March 13, 1774. p. 156

Machen, John, son of William and Sarah. Born February 27 and Baptized
April 2, 1769. p. 35

Machen, Judith, daughter of Samuel and Ann. Born February 8 and Baptized
March 5, 1769. p. 35

Machen, Lettitia, daughter of Samuel and Ann. Born November 4 and
Baptized December 4, 1763. p. 26

Machen, Mary, daughter of John and Mary. Born January 21 and Baptized
March 3, 1771. p. 38

Machen, Mary, daughter of William and Sarah. Born April 16 and Baptized
May 19, 1765. p. 28

Machen, Nancy, daughter of Robert and Ann. Born January 8 and Baptized
March 1, 1772. p. 40

Machen, Nanny, daughter of Samuel and Nanny. Born July 13 and Baptized
September 20, 1767. p. 32

Machen, Patty, daughter of Samuel and Ann. Born April 16 and Baptized
June 16, 1765. p. 28

Machen, Peggy, daughter of John and Mary. Born April 26 and Baptized
June 4, 1777. p. 165

Machen, Richard, son of Robert and Ann. Born April 4 and Baptized
September 3, 1769. p. 36

Machen, Richard, son of William and Sarah. Born May 26 and Baptized
July 8, 1760. p. 20

Machen, Sally, daughter of William and Sarah. Born May 7 and Baptized
June 31, 1767. p. 32

Machen, Susannah, daughter of Robert and Ann. Born September 27 and
Baptized November 4, 1764. p. 28

Machen, Thomas, son of John and Mary. Born _____, 1774 and Baptized
April 6, 1774. p. 156

Machen, William, son of William and Sarah. Born January 11 and Baptized
February 13, 1763. p. 24

Machen, _____ny, daughter of Samuel and Nanny. Baptized December 31,
1776. p. 163

Manuel, Milly, bastard daughter of Elizabeth Manuel. Born April 2 and
Baptized May 15, 1757. p. 14

Marchant, Ann, daughter of John and Esther. Born October __, 1770 and
Baptized December 9, 1770. p. 38

Marchant, Charlotte, Sp. daughter of Elizabeth Marchant. Born October 17 and Baptized December 5, 1773. p. 155

Marchant, Christopher, son of Edmund and Elizabeth. Born November 22 and Baptized December 22, 1771. p. 40

Marchant, Christopher, son of Richard and Ann. Born March 27 and Baptized May 9, 1762. p. 22

Marchant, Elisha, son of Elisha and Esther. Born June 16 and Baptized July 17, 1774. p. 157

Marchant, Mary, daughter of Abraham and Ann. Born November 28, 1762 and Baptized January 30, 1763. p. 24

Marchant, Mary, daughter of Richard and Ann. Born September 4 and Baptized October 14, 1770. p. 37

Marchant, Richard, son of Elisha and Esther. Born June 7 and Baptized July 8, 1770. p. 37

Marchant, Richard Bartlet, son of Edmund and Elizabeth. Born May 7 and Baptized June 5, 1774. p. 156

Marchant, William Fordham, Sp. son of Joyce Marchant. Born January 29 and Baptized February 27, 1774. p. 156

Mason, Mary, daughter of Thomas and Elizabeth. Baptized November 17, 1776. p. 163

Matthews, John Edwards, son of Robert and Ann. Born August 9 and Baptized September 15, 1774. p. 157

Matthews, Nancy Thornton, daughter of Robert and _____. Baptized December 30, 1776. p. 163

Mecoy, Francis, son of Charles and Johannah. Born August 8 and Baptized October 9, 1763. p. 26

Mecoy, Charles, son of Charles and Johannah. Born September 17 and Baptized October 27, 1765. p. 29

Meggs, John, son of John and Sarah. Born March 11 and Baptized April 21, 1776. p. 162

Megs, Jenny, daughter of John and Sarah. Born July 11 and Baptized July 24, 1768. p. 34

Megs, Nancy, daughter of John and Sarah. Born March 26 and Baptized April 29, 1770. p. 36

Megs, Thomas, son of John and Sarah. Born August 8 and Baptized September 13, 1772. p. 151

Merchant, Abraham, son of Ambrose and Elizabeth. Born March 7 and
Baptized April 5, 1760. p. 19

Merchant, Ambrose, son of Richard and Ann. Born November 18 and
Baptized December 20, 1772. p. 152

Merchant, Elizabeth Adams, daughter of Edmund and _____. Baptized
February 9, 1777. p. 164

Merchant, John, son of Richard and Ann. Baptized March 5, 1775. p. 158

Merchant, Lucy, daughter of Richard and Ann. Born March 1 and Baptized
May 1, 1757. p. 14

Merchant, Richard, son of Richard and Joyce. Born December 8, 1775 and
Baptized February 7, 1776. p. 161

Merchant, Sarah, daughter of William and Ann. Baptized October 4, 1772.
p. 151

Merchant, William, son of Richard and Ann. Born September 10, ___. p. C

Michael, Judith, daughter of Edward and Joyce. Born October 2 and
Baptized November 9, 1760. p. 20

Michel, Ann, daughter of Edward and Joyce. Born May 28 and Baptized
June 26, 1757. p. 14

Michel, John, son of Fdward and Joyce. Born October 29, 1763. p. 26

Miller, Ann, daughter of Gabriel and Mary. Born September 5 and Baptized
October 17, 1756. p. 13

Miller, Ann, daughter of Joseph and Sarah. Born September 28 and Baptized
October 28, 1759. p. 18

Miller, Averilla, daughter of Gabriel and Mary. Born August 9 and
Baptized September 3, 1769. p. 36

Miller, Betty, daughter of Gabriel and Mary. Born December 26, 1762 and
Baptized March 30, 1763. p. 24

Miller, Betty, daughter of John and Judith. Born April 27 and Baptized
June 8, 1760. p. 20

Miller, Booker, son of Gabriel and Betsy. Born December 28, 1793. p.174

Miller, Catherine, daughter of Francis and Avy. Born August 5, 1780. p.171

Miller, Caty, daughter of Joseph and Sarah. Born March 20 and Baptized
April 29, 1770. p. 36

Miller, Ferdelia, daughter of Gabriel and Betsy. Born February 6, 1796.
p. 175

Miller, Francis, son of Gabriel and Betsy. Born August 27, 1798. p. 176

Miller, Francis, son of Isaac and Elizabeth. Born October 16 and Baptized December 18, 1763. p. 26

Miller, Francis, son of Joseph and Sarah. Born October 27 and Baptized December 11, 1757. p. 15

Miller, Gabriel, son of Gabriel and Mary. Born October 31, 1766. p. 31

Miller, Isaac, son of Isaac and Elizabeth. Born March 31 and Baptized April 16, 1769. p. 35

Miller, Jenny Dudley, daughter of Anderson and Dorothy. Born January 8 and Baptized February 5, 1775. p. 158

Miller, Joanna, daughter of Gabriel and Mary. Born March 6 and Baptized May 11, 1760. p. 19

Miller, John, son of Francis and Franky. Born November 3 and Baptized December 17, 1775. p. 160

Miller, John, son of Francis and Averilla. Born March 25 and Baptized April 20, 1777. p. 164

Miller, Joseph, son of John and Judith. Born April 2 and Baptized May 15, 1757. p. 14

Miller, Joseph, son of Joseph and Sarah. Born August 6 and Baptized October 9, 1763. p. 26

Miller, Martha, daughter of Joseph and Sarah. Born April 19 and Baptized May 9, 1773. p. 153

Miller, Mary, daughter of John and Judith. Born May 27 and Baptized July 29, 1764. p. 27

Miller, Mary, daughter of Joseph and Sarah. Born April 30 and Baptized June 1, 1777. p. 165

Miller, Nancy, daughter of Joseph and Sarah. Born May 5 and Baptized June 12, 1768. p. 33

Miller, Nanny, daughter of James and Ann. Born June 13 and Baptized November 29, 1767. p. 32

Miller, Polly, daughter of Gabriel and Betsey. Born _____ 1792. p. 174

Miller, Rebekah, daughter of James and Ann. Born July 7 and Baptized August 2, 1770. p. 37

Miller, Roseannah, daughter of Isaac and Elizabeth. Born July 7, 1765. p. 29

Miller, Sally, daughter of Gabriel and Mary. Born March 21 and Baptized
    May 9, 1773. p. 153

Miller, Sarah, daughter of Joseph and Sarah. Born August 30 and Baptized
    October 20, 1765. p. 29

Miller, Seth Foster, son of Gabriel and Betsy. Born March 31, 1801. p.176

Miller, Whitney, a bastard son of Ann Miller. Born February 26, 1770. p.36

Minter, Anne, daughter of William and Judith. Born April 30, 1763. p. 25

Minter, Anthony, son of John and _____. Baptized March 23, 1776. p. 162

Minter, Anthony, son of William and Judith. Born July 5 and Baptized
    August 22, 1756. p. 12

Minter, Francis, son of John and Ann. Born May 29 and Baptized June 25,
    1769. p. 35

Minter, James, son of James and Ann. Born November 6 and Baptized
    December 17, 1775. p. 161

Minter, James, son of John and Ann. Born January 18 and Baptized
    March 1, 1772. p. 40

Minter, John, son of John and Ann. Born May 20 and Baptized June 15,
    1777. p. 165

Minter, Josiah, son of James and Ann. Born June 22 and Baptized
    June 24, 1770. p. 37

Minter, Joyce, daughter of William and Judith. Born July 14 and Baptized
    August 19, 1759. p. 18

Minter, Judith, daughter of John and Ann. Born March 26 and Baptized
    May 8, 1774. p. 156

Minter, Judith, daughter of William and Mary. Born February 1 and
    Baptized February 26, 1775. p. 158

Minter, Thomas, son of James and Ann. Born October 15 and Baptized
    October 24, 1773. p. 154

Minter, William, son of John and Ann. Born December 27, 1767 and Baptized
    February 21, 1768. p. 33

Minter, William, son of William and Mary. Born September 15, 1788. p.173

Mitchel, Cyrum, daughter of James and Sarah S. Born June 3, 1808. p. 177

Mitchel, Mordecai, son of James C. and Sarah S. Born January 25, 1810.
    p. 177

Mitchell, Johannah, daughter of Edward and Joyce. Born August 6 and
      Baptized September 20, 1773. p. 154

Montgommery, Leroy, son of David and Ann. Born September 30, 1766 and
      Baptized January 11, 1767. p. 31

Morgan, Betty, daughter of Benjamin and Mary. Born November 10, 1758. p.17

Morgan, Betsy, daughter of James and Elizabeth. Born November 27, 1772. p.152

Morgan, Forrest, son of James and Elizabeth. Born May 18 and Baptized
      June 29, 1766. p. 30

Morgan, Franky, daughter of Richard and Ann. Born December 19, 1775 and
      Baptized March 10, 1776. p. 161

Morgan, George, son of James and Elizabeth. Born April 16 and Baptized
      June 28, 1769. p. 35

Morgan, James, son of Mark and Ann. Born November 11 and Baptized
      December 29, 1775. p. 161

Morgan, John, son of James and Elizabeth. Born November 16, 1758 and
      Baptized January 21, 1759. p. 17

Morgan, John, son of Mark and Ann. Born November 15 and Baptized December 27,
      1767. p. 33

Morgan, John Howard, son of William and Ann. Born October 19 and Baptized
      November 18, 1764. p. 28

Morgan, Joshua, son of Benjamin and Mary. Born January 7 and Baptized
      February 27, 1774. p. 156

Morgan, Judith, daughter of Benjamin and Mary. Born September 7 and
      Baptized October 13, 1771. p. 39

Morgan, Judith, daughter of James and Elizabeth. Born November 6 and
      Baptized December 12, 1756. p. 13

Morgan, Mary, daughter of Benjamin and Mary. Born October 7 and Baptized
      November 8, 1761. p. 22

Morgan, Nancy, daughter of Richard and Ann. Born April 7 and Baptized
      May 9, 1773. p. 153

Morgan, Nanny, daughter of Ben and Mary. Born February 27 and Baptized
      May 4, 1766. p. 30

Morgan, Richard, son of Mark and Ann. Born July 31 and Baptized August 31,
      1777. p. 165

Morgan, Sarah, daughter of Richard and Ann. Born June 12 and Baptized
July 8, 1770. p. 37

Morgan, Suky, daughter of Benjamin and Mary. Born September 15 and
Baptized November 13, 1768. p. 34

Morgan, Thomas, son of James and Elisabeth. Born August 21 and Baptized
September 4, 1777. p. 165

Morgan, William, son of Benjamin and Mary. Born March 29 and Baptized
May 20, 1764. p. 27

Morgan, William, son of James and Elizabeth. Born February 9 and
Baptized March 28, 1762. p. 22

Morgan, _____, daughter of James and Elisabeth. Baptized March 9,
1755. p. D

Morgan, _____, child of John and Ann. p. A

Morris, Ann, daughter of John and Mary. Born May 27 and Baptized
June 27, 1767. p. 32

Morris, Elizabeth, daughter of John and Mary. Born August 15 and
Baptized September 16, 1770. p. 37

Morris, John, son of John and Mary. Born January 26 and Baptized
February 28, 1773. p. 152

Morris, Lucy, daughter of John and Mary. Born March 8, 1769. p. 35

Morris, Thomas, son of John and Mary. Born April 16 and Baptized
May 28, 1775. p. 159

Morris, William, son of John and Mary. Born July 6 and Baptized
August 11, 1765. p. 29

Mullikin, Katy, Sp. daughter of Ann Colman. Born January 17 and
Baptized February 20, 1774. p. 155

N

Newburn, Jimmy, son of Thomas and Joyce. Born June 9 and Baptized
August 3, 1760. p. 20

Newburn, Michael Terril, son of Thomas and Mary. Born October 20,
1794. p. 174

Newburn, Thomas, son of Thomas and Joyce. Born February 16 and
Baptized April 14, 1771. p. 39

Newburn, Thomas Foster, son of Thomas and Mary. Born March 20, 1796.
p. 175

Newel, John, son of William and Sarah. Born September 24 and Baptized
 November 11, 1759. p. 18

Norris, Thomas, son of Joseph and Elizabeth. Born November 22 and Baptized
 December 9, 1770. p. 38

Nottingham, Esther, daughter of Richard and Sarah. Baptized May 4, 1777.
 p. 164

O

Oliver, Armistead, son of Gravely and Judith. Born August 4, 1759. p. 18

Oliver, Sarah, daughter of Graveley and Judith. Born October 10, 1766. p. 31

Over, John Powel, a bastard son of Elizabeth. Born December 18, 1765 and
 Baptized January 26, 1766. p. 29

Owen, Anna Boss, a bastard daughter of Sally Owen. Born March 1 and Baptized
 March 29, 1772. p. 40

Owen, Armistead Lewis, son of George and Lucrecia. Born June 27, 1796.
 p. 175

Owen, Betsey, daughter of George and Joanna. Born October 6 and Baptized
 November 6, 1774. p. 157

Owen, Betty, daughter of Edmond and Elizabeth. Born June 16 and Baptized
 July 4, 1762. p. 23

Owen, Christopher, son of George and Lucretia. Born March 22, 1799. p. 176

Owen, Dorothy, daughter of George and _____. Born September __, 1776 and
 Baptized October 16, 1776. p. 163

Owen, Edmund, son of Edmund and Elizabeth. Born March 12 and Baptized
 May 4, 1766. p. 30

Owen, Elizabeth, daughter of William and Ann. Born April 17 and Baptized
 May 15, 1757. p. 14

Owen, Frankey, daughter of George and Joanna. Born March 29 and Baptized
 May 1, 1757. p. 14

Owen, George, son of Edmond and Elizabeth. Born May 25 and Baptized
 July 1, 1764. p. 27

Owen, George, son of George and Johanna. Born August 5 and Baptized
 September 9, 1764. p. 27

Owen, Joanna, daughter of George and Joanna. Born April 4, 1760. p. 20

Owen, Joanna, daughter of William and Ann. Born May 4 and Baptized
June 24, 1759. p. 18

Owen, John, son of Edmond and Elizabeth. Born June 4 and Baptized
June 27, 1756. p. 12

Owen, John, son of William and Susannah. Born February 24 and Baptized
April 8, 1764. p. 27

Owen, Joyce Forrest, daughter of George and Joanna. Born February 20,
and Baptized March 29, 1772. p. 40

Owen, Joyce, daughter of William and Susanna. Born June 19 and Baptized
July 23, 1769. p. 35

Owen, Mary, daughter of Edmond and Elizabeth. Born January 2 and Baptized
February 17, 1760. p. 19

Owen, Mary, daughter of William and Ann. Born July 26 and Baptized
August 2, 1755. p. 11

Owen, Mary, daughter of William and Susanna. Baptized July 16, 1775. p.160

Owen, Molly, daughter of George and Joanna. Born April 23 and Baptized
May 23, 1762. p. 23

Owen, Nanny, daughter of George and Joanna. Born March 28 and Baptized
May 17, 1765. p. 32

Owen, Sarah, daughter of William and Susanna. Born December 11, 1761 and
Baptized January 31, 1762. p. 22

Owen, Susanna, daughter of William and Susanna. Born ____, 1773 and
Baptized May 23, 1773. p. 153

Owen, Thomas Forrest, son of George and Joanna. Born April 22, 1769. p.35

Owen, William, son of William and Susannah. Born June 27 and Baptized
August 10, 1766. p. 30

Owen, _____, son of George and Joannah. Born May __, 1755 and
Baptized July 13, 1755. p. 11

P

Pallister, John, son of John and Mary. Born February 1 and Baptized
April 13, 1777. p. 164

Palmer, Gwyn Read, son of Nathaniel and Lucy. Born October 10, 1763.
p. 26

Parrot, Augustine, son of John and Sarah. Born September 30 and Baptized
November 9, 1777. p. 166

Parrot, Elizabeth, daughter of Richard and Susanna. Born June 8, 1780. p.171

Parrot, Joseph, son of Robert and Elizabeth. Born November 3 and Baptized December 18, 1775. p. 161

Parrot, Machen, son of Richard and Susanna. Born July 10 and Baptized September 3, 1777. p. 165

Parsons, Absalom, son of John and Mary. Born June 10, 1768. p. 34

Parsons, Bathsheba, daughter of John and Mary. Born May 1 and Baptized June 17, 1775. p. 159

Parsons, Betty, daughter of John and Mary. Born September 19 and Baptized October 19, 1766. p. 31

Parsons, Judith, daughter of James and Caty. Born November 1 and Baptized November 22, 1772. p. 152

Parsons, Mary, daughter of James and Judith. Born April 4 and Baptized April 30, 1769. p. 35

Parsons, Mary, daughter of John and Mary. Born September __, 1770 and Baptized October 14, 1770. p. 37

Parsons, Sally, daughter of John and Mary. Born April 23 and Baptized May 23, 1773. p. 153

Pead, Fanny Cymer, daughter of Hunley and Mary. Born November 7, 1782. p.171

Pead, James, son of Hundley and Mary. Born September 5, 1780. p. 171

Peade, Ann, daughter of Lewis and Mary. Born August 7 and Baptized August 27, 1775. p. 160

Peade, George, son of John and Susanna. Born April 20 and Baptized May 21, 1777. p. 165

Peade, Lewis, son of James and Sally. Born February 16 and Baptized March 24, 1776. p. 162

Peade, Thomas, son of John and Susanna. Born January 4 and Baptized February 26, 1775. p. 158

Peak, Robert, son of Thomas and Dorothy. Baptized September 8, 1776. p.163

Peak, William, son of Thomas and Elizabeth. Born October 29 and Baptized November 28, 1756. p. 13

Peak, Lydia, daughter of William and Annah. Born December 18, 1775 and Baptized March 10, 1776. p. 161

Peed, Ann, daughter of James and Priscilla. Born July 19, 1755. p. 11 (see Hunley Peed)

Peed, Ann, daughter of John and Elizabeth. Born April 21 and Baptized
    June 19, 1763. p. 25

Peed, _____, daughter of George and Elizabeth. Baptized March __, 1755.
    p. D

Peed, Dolly, daughter of George and Elizabeth. Born December 26, 1762
    and Baptized February 13, 1763. p. 24

Peed, Elias, son of Philip and Elizabeth. Born December 25, 1765 and
    Baptized January 26, 1766. p. 29

Peed, Elizabeth, daughter of George and Elizabeth. Born January 15, 1761.
    p. 21

Peed, Elizabeth, daughter of Philip and Elizabeth. Born April 15, and
    Baptized May 15, 1768. p. 33

Peed, George, son of George and Elizabeth. Born January 28 and Baptized
    March 9, 1766. p. 30

Peed, Humphry, son of George and Elizabeth. Born December 15, 1758 and
    Baptized January 21, 1759. p. 17

Peed, Hundley, son of James and Priscilla. Born July 20, 1755. p. 11
    (See Ann Peed, page 90)

Peed, James, son of Philip and Dorothy. Born May 18 and Baptized
    June 13, 1773. p. 154

Peed, James, son of William and Mary. Born December 9, 1768. p. 34

Peed, John, son of James and Priscilla. Born April 29 and Baptized
    May 28, 1758. p. 16

Peed, John, son of John and Elizabeth. Born November 29, 1760 and
    Baptized January 18, 1761. p. 20

Peed, John, son of Philip and Dorothy. Born September 6 and Baptized
    October 29, 1769. p. 36

Peed, John, son of William and Mary. Born June 26 and Baptized July 19,
    1761. p. 21

Peed, Joseph, son of George and Elizabeth. Born April 18 and Baptized
    April 29, 1770. p. 37

Peed, Mary, daughter of James and Priscilla. Born March 2 and Baptized
    April 8, 1764. p. 27

Peed, Milley, a bastard daughter of Mary Peed. Born May 28 and Baptized
    June 16, 1765. p. 28

Peed, Nancy, daughter of Philip and Elizabeth. Born December 20, 1760 and Baptized February 1, 1761. p. 21

Peed, Patty, daughter of Philip and Elizabeth. Born October 13, 1763. p. 26

Peed, Peggy, daughter of George and Elizabeth. Born December 25, 1756. p. 13

Peed, Philip, son of Philip and Elizabeth. Born April 12 and Baptized May 24, 1772. p. 151

Peed, Richard, son of Lewis and Ann. Born February 8 and Baptized March 9, 1766. p. 30

Peed, Robert Hunley, son of William and Mary. Born July 17 and Baptized August 19, 1772. p. 151

Peed, Sarah, daughter of James and Priscilla. Born March 8, 1760. p.19

Peed, Uriah, son of Lewis and Ann. Born April 5 and Baptized May 13, 1759. p. 17

Peed, William, son of John and Elizabeth. Born September 1 and Baptized October 12, 1758. p. 16

Peed, William, son of Lewis and Ann. Born February 1 and Baptized March 20, 1757. p. 14

Peed, William, son of Mary Bridge "begotten as she sayeth by Philip Peed." Born September 4 and Baptized December 4, 1763. p.26

Peed, William, son of William and Mary. Born February 4 and Baptized March 9, 1765. p. 28

Perrot, Fanny, daughter of John and Sarah. Born January 9 and Baptized February 10, 1776. p. 161

Perrot, George, son of George and Lucy. Born July 7 and Baptized August 7, 1774. p. 157

Perrot, George Nevil, son of Richard and Susanna. Born January 30, and Baptized March 19, 1775. p. 158

Perrot, George, son of Robert and _____. Born March 2 and Baptized April 4, 1773. p. 153

Perrot, James, son of John and Elizabeth. Born July 2 and Baptized August 7, 1774. p. 157

Perrot, Joanna, daughter of John and Elisabeth. Born January 14, and Baptized March 16, 1777. p. 164

Perrot, Robert, son of George and Lucy. Born ____ 1771 and Baptized
April 21, 1771. p. 39

Perrot, Robert, son of Richard and _____. Baptized November 3, 1771.
p. 151

Peterson, Alice, daughter of Peter and Mary. Born February 22 and
Baptized May 17, 1771. p. 39

Peterson, Caty, daughter of Peter and Mary. Born February 27 and
Baptized April 2, 1769. p. 35

Pew, _____as, son of William and Johannah. Born June __, 1755 and
Baptized July 13, 1755. p. 11

Pew, Joanna, daughter of William and Joanna. Born November 20 and
Baptized December 27, 1767. p. 33

Pew, Josiah, son of William and Joanna. Born June __, 1762 and Baptized
July 18, 1762. p. 23

Pew, Mary, daughter of William and Ann. Born April 11, 1788. p. 173

Pew, Sarah, daughter of William and Johannah. Born September 24 and
Baptized October 28, 1759. p. 18

Pew, William, son of William and Johannah. Born December 14, 1756 and
Baptized January 23, 1757. p. 13

Peyton, Elizabeth, daughter of (Sir) John and Frances. Born February 6,
1756. p. 12

Peyton, Harriot, daughter of (Sir) John and Francis. Born February 19,
1761. p. 21

Peyton, Henry Yelverton, son of (Sir) John and Frances. Born May 5
and Baptized June 5, 1770. p. 37

Peyton, Martha Cook, daughter of (Sir) John and Frances. Born March 13,
1763. p. 25

Peyton, Mary, daughter of (Sir) John and Frances. Born June 11, 1758.
p. 16

Peyton, Seignora, daughter of (Sir) John and Frances. Born January 8,
1767. p. 31

Plummer, Judith, daughter of Kemp and Judith. p. A

Plummer, Thomas, son of George and Margaret. Baptized December 4, 1774.
p. 157

Plummer, Thomas, son of George and Margaret. Born November 5, 1774 and
Baptized January 1, 1775. p. 158

Pool, Robert, son of Robert and Susannah. Born December 26, 1757 and Baptized February 5, 1758. p. 15

Powel, Betty, daughter of John and Elizabeth. Born December 25, 1763 and Baptized February 12, 1764. p. 26

Powel, Edmond, son of John and Elizabeth. Born February __, 1765. p. 28

Powel, Joanna, daughter of John and Elizabeth. Born April 17 and Baptized June 12, 1768. p. 33

Powel, Mary, daughter of John and Elizabeth. Born May 12 and Baptized June 20, 1762. p. 23

Powel, Mildred, daughter of John and Elizabeth. Born August 23 and Baptized September 26, 1773. p. 154

Powel, Rosannah, daughter of Henry and Mary. Born June 20 and Baptized July 13, 1766. p. 30

Powell, John, son of Henry and Mary. Born August 22, 1755. p. 11

Powell, William, son of Henry and Mary. Born July 7 and Baptized July 31, 1763. p. 25

Powers, Salley, daughter of John and Sarah. Born August 1 and Baptized August 31, 1760. p. 20

Presley, William, son of John and Mary. Born December 5, 1765 and Baptized January 12, 1766. p. 29

Pritchard, Henry and Robert, twin sons of John and Hannah. Baptized November 25, 1776. p. 163

Pritchard, William Lucas, son of John and Joyce. Born June 7 and Baptized June 8, 1773. p. 154

Pugh, William Forrest, son of Elias and Susanna. Born October 1 and Baptized November 2, 1777. p. 166

Purcell, Elizabeth, daughter of James and Elizabeth. Born August 20 and Baptized September 12, 1773. p. 154

Q

Quin, Sally, daughter of Peter and Mary. Born March 23, 1757. p. 14

Quin, Elizabeth White, Sp. daughter of Sarah Quin. Born January 8 and Baptized March 3, 1776. p. 161

R

Ranson, Lettitia, daughter of James and Lettitia. Born April 13 and Baptized May 23, 1762. p. 23

Ransone, Ann, daughter of James and Lettitia. Born December 26, 1756. p. 13

Ransone, (Jam)es, son of James and Lettitia. Born May __, 1755. p. 11

Ransone, Lucy, daughter of James and Lettitia. Born April 20, 1764. p.27

Ransone, Matthew James, son of Richard and Ann. Born December 25, 1773 and Baptized February 5, 1774. p. 155

Ransone, Robert, son of James and Lettitia. Born December 29, 1758. p.17

Ransone, Sarah, daughter of James and Lettitia. Born March 15, 1760. p. 19

Read, Dorothy, daughter of Gwyn and Mary. Born August 1, and Baptized September 12, 1774. p. 157

Reade, Dorothy Clock, daughter of James and Sarah. Born August 12 and Baptized September 9, 1770. p. 37

Reade, Gwyn, son of John and Judith. Born March 1 and Baptized March 3, 1772. p. 40

Reade, James, son of James and Sarah. Baptized May 19, 1777. p. 165

Reade, Judith Armistead, daughter of John and Judith. Born April 8 and Baptized May 20, 1770. p. 37

Reade, William, son of Gwyn and Dorothy. Born October 25, 1758. p. 17

Repress, Lucy, daughter of Richard and Lucy. Born February 13 and Baptized February 18, 1773. p. 152

Respess, Elizabeth, daughter of Thomas and Ann. Born September 22 and Baptized December 11, 1768. p. 34

Respess, Elliot, son of Thomas and _____. Baptized December 13, 1772. p. 152

Respess, John, son of Richard and Lucy. Born January 1 and Baptized February 5, 1758. p. 16

Respess, Lucy, daughter of Richard and Lucy. Born November 16 and Baptized December 18, 1774. p. 158

Respess, Lucy, daughter of Robert and _____. Baptized July 7, 1776. p. 162

Respess, Machen, son of Thomas and Susanna. Born _____ 1772 and Baptized January 10, 1773. p. 152

Respess, Mary, daughter of Robert and Elizabeth. Born June 9 and Baptized July 19, 1774. p. 157

Respess, Matthew, son of Richard and Lucy. Born March 12, 1764. p. 27

Respess, Richard, son of Richard and Lucy. Born February 2 and Baptized April 5, 1760. p. 19

Respess, Thomas, son of Thomas and Mary. Baptized January 21, 1776. p.161

Reynolds, John, son of John and _____. Baptized October 26, 1777. p.166

Reynolds, Sally, Spurious daughter of Dorothy Reynolds. Baptized March 19, 1775. p. 158

Reynolds, William Younger, son of William and Catherine. Born May 31, and Baptized July 6, 1777. p. 165

Ripley, Fanny, daughter of Thomas and Mary. Born March 1, 1794. p. 174

Ripley, John, son of Thomas and Mary. Born May 6, 1796. p. 175

Ripley, Judith and William, bastard twins of Richard Ripley and Sarah Owen. Born October 27, 1786. p. 172

Ripley, Lucy, daughter of Thomas and Mary. Born May 25, 1790. p. 173

Ripley, Philip, son of John and Deborah. Born May 13 and Baptized June 22, 1760. p. 20

Ripley, Thomas, son of Thomas and Mary. Born February 27, 1792. p. 174

Riply, Andrew, son of John and Deborah. Born March 3 and Baptized May 1, 1757. p. 14

Robins, Alban, son of Edmund and Ann. Born April 24 and Baptized May 20, 1775. p. 159

Robins, Betsy, daughter of John and Judith. Born November 17, 1799. p.176

Robins, Edmond Lewis, son of James and Elizabeth. Born March 1, 1794. p.174

Robins, Elisabeth, daughter of Peter and Elisabeth. Born June 16 and Baptized July 21, 1777. p. 165

Robins, Elizabeth, daughter of Alban and Annah. Born October __, 1766 and Baptized November 30, 1766. p. 31

Robins, George William, son of William and Mary. Born February 12 and Baptized April 25, 1773. p. 153

Robins, James, son of Edmund and Ann. Born August 16 and Baptized September 18, 1768. p. 34

Robins, James, son of James and Joanna. Born October 9, 1808. p.177

Robins, James, son of John and Judith. Born August 14, 1789. p.173

Robins, John, son of Edmund and Ann. Born December 18, 1765 and Baptized January 26, 1766. p. 29

Robins, John, son of Peter and Elizabeth. Born February 2 and Baptized May 1, 1768. p. 33

Robins, John, son of William and Mary. Born April 10 and Baptized May 4, 1766. p. 30

Robins, Letitia, daughter of Edmund and Ann. Born August 1, 1777. p.165

Robins, Lucretia, daughter of James and Joanna. Born August 27, 1806. p. 177

Robins, Mary, daughter of Alban and Anna. Born July 29, 1770. p. 37

Robins, Mary, daughter of Edmond and Ann. Born November 20, 1760 and Baptized January 4, 1761. p. 20

Robins, Mary, daughter of Peter and Elizabeth. Born September __, 1772 and Baptized October 11, 1772. p. 151

Robins, Milly, daughter of Alban and Ann_er_. Born August 6 and Baptized September 11, 1774. p. 157

Robins, Nancy, daughter of Alban and Anna. Born _____1771 and Baptized December 9, 1771. p. 40

Robins, Nancy, daughter of John and Judith. Born September 2, 1787. p.172

Robins, Nancy Soper, daughter of James and Elizabeth. Born April 12, 1799. p. 1799. p. 176

Robins, Polly, daughter of James and Elizabeth. Born September 8, 1796. p. 175

Robins, Robert, son of Peter and Elizabeth. Born March 15 and Baptized April 29, 1770. p. 36

Robins, Sarah, daughter of Alban and Anna_h_. Born May 17 and Baptized June 26, 1768. p. 33

Robins, Susanna, daughter of John and Judith. Born July 28, 1797. p.175

Robins, Thomas, son of Peter and Elizabeth. Born February 21 and Baptized March 26, 1775. p. 158

Robins, Thomas, son of William and Mary. Born November 6 and Baptized December 11, 1768. p. 34

Robins, William, son of Alban and Mary. Born June 14 and Baptized July 3, 1763. p. 25

Robins, William, son of Peter and Elizabeth. Born March 10 and Baptized May 4, 1766. p. 30

Robinson, Peter, son of Major John Robinson and Mary. Born September 23, 1766. p. 31

Rogers, Mary, daughter of Thomas and Ann. Born March 9 and Baptized April 10, 1773. p. 153

Ruff, John, son of John and Ann. Baptized December 12, 1773. p. 155

Ruff, Sally, daughter of John and Ann. Born August 3, 1766. p. 31

R_____, _____, child of Robert and Margaret. Baptized 1755. p. D

S

Sadler, Ann, daughter of Thomas and Mary. Born March 30 and Baptized May 10, 1772. p. 40

Sadler, Averilla, daughter of William and Ann. Born February 7 and Baptized March 13, 1774. p. 156

Sadler, Betty, daughter of Robert and Sarah. Born October 22 and Baptized November 12, 1769. p. 36

Sadler, Edward, son of Robert and Margaret. Born October 2 and Baptized November 28, 1773. p. 155

Sadler, Henry Atherton, son of Robert and Margaret. Born March 24 and April 27, 1777. p. 164

Sadler, Jesse, son of Thomas and Mary. Born December 9, 1773 and Baptized February 27, 1774. p. 155

Sadler, John, son of William and Ann. Born October 21 and Baptized November 13, 1768. p. 34

Sadler, Micael, son of Robert and Sarah. Born December 24, 1764 and Baptized March 10, 1765. p. 28

Sadler, Robert, son of Robert and Sarah. Born November __, 1757 and Baptized December 11, 1757. p. 15

Sadler, Robert, son of Robert and Sarah. Born December 23, 1759 and Baptized February 3, 1760. p. 19

Sadler, Susanna, daughter of Thomas and Mary. Born February 10 and Baptized March 24, 1776. p. 162

Sadler, William, son of Robert and Sarah. Born September 13 and Baptized
    October 24, 1762. p. 24

Sadler, William, son of William and Ann. Born January 19 and Baptized
    March 3, 1771. p. 38

Sampson, James, son of John and Elizabeth. Born May 15 and Baptized
    June 19, 1763. p. 25

Sampson, John, son of John and Elizabeth. Born September 28, 1765. p.29

Sampson, Nancy, daughter of Thomas (deceased) and Joyce. Born August 20
    and Baptized September 8, 1773. p. 154

Sampson, Stephen, son of John and Elizabeth. Born October 4 and Baptized
    October 5, 1771. p. 39

Sampson, Thomas, son of John and Elizabeth. Born November 6, 1772 and
    Baptized January 3, 1773. p. 152

Sanders, John, son of John and Rebecca. Born June 6 and Baptized
    August 3, 1760. p. 20

Sandy, Elizabeth, daughter of William and _____. Baptized July 2, 1775.
    p. 159

Saunders, John, son of Thomas and Ann. Born February 19 and Baptized
    March 22, 1774. p. 156

Sellers, Ann and Sarah, daughters of Thomas and Ann. Born February 8,
    1761. p. 21

Sellers, Betty, daughter of Thomas and Ann. Born September 24 and
    Baptized October 23, 1763. p. 26

Sellers, Mary, daughter of Thomas and Ann. Born June 24 and Baptized
    July 25, 1756. p. 12

Sellers, William, son of Thomas and Ann. Born October 1 and Baptized
    October 19, 1758. p. 17

Shackelford, Charles, son of Benjamin and Martha. Born December 17,
    1773 and Baptized January 29, 1774. p. 155

Shackelford, Maria, daughter of Benjamin and Martha. Born January 18
    and Baptized February 18, 1776. p. 161

Shipley, Ann, daughter of Joseph and _____. Baptized December 1, 1776.
    p. 163

Shipley, George, son of Joseph and Jane. Born June 2 and Baptized
    July 1, 1764. p. 27

Shipley, Joseph, son of Ralph and Joyce. Born September 20 and Baptized November 18, 1764. p. 28

Shipley, Mary, daughter of Joseph and Jane. Born May 26 and Baptized July 5, 1772. p. 151

Shipley, Mildred, daughter of Ralph and Joyce. Born November 20, 1776 and Baptized January 23, 1777. p. 164

Shipley, Richard, son of Ralph and Joyce. Born September 20 and Baptized October 29, 1769. p. 36

Shipley, Susanna, daughter of Ralph and Joyce. Born October 27 and Baptized December 5, 1773. p. 155

Shiply, George, son of Ralph and Joyce. Born July 17 and Baptized August 9, 1767. p. 32

Shurles, R_elph, son of Robert and Mary. Born February 6, 1757. p. 14

Simmons, Ann, daughter of Anthony and Joanna. Born June 1, 1792. p. 174

Simmons, Ann, daughter of William and Ann. Born November 14, 1775 and Baptized January 14, 1776. p. 161

Simmons, Anthony, son of William and Ann. Born April 4 and Baptized May 13, 1770. p. 37

Simmons, Betsy, daughter of William and Ann. Born March 6 and Baptized April 10, 1774. p. 156

Simmons, Mary, daughter of William and Ann. Born October 23 and Baptized December 14, 1777. p. 166

Simmons, William, son of Anthony and Joanna. Born October 29, 1793. p. 174

Simmons, William, son of William and Ann. Born February 18 and Baptized March 29, 1772. p. 40

Singleton, _____, son of Isaac and Jean. p. A

Singleton, (Ant)hony, son of Henry and Lettitia. Born ____ 1755. p. D

Singleton, John, son of Anthony and Ann. Born July 2, 1758 and Baptized August _____. p. 16

Singleton, Pemmy, daughter of Henry and Pemmy. Born March 7 and Baptized May 9, 1762. p. 22

Singleton, William, son of Richard and Averilla. Born October 2 and Baptized October 24, 1762. p. 24

Smith, Armistead, son of Thomas and Dorothy. Born December 1, 1756. p.13

Smith, Ann, daughter of Isaac and Judith. Born June 16 and Baptized
July 28, 1776. p. 163

Smith, Ann, daughter of Peter and Bathsheba. Born July 11 and Baptized
August 14, 1763. p. 25

Smith, Baldwin, son of William and Elizabeth. Baptized February 3, 1778.
p. 171

Smith, Betty, daughter of Peter and Bathsheba. Born June 16 and Baptized
July 13, 1755. p. 11

Smith, Elisabeth, daughter of William and Bathsheba. Born March 30 and
Baptized May 4, 1777. p. 164

Smith, Elizabeth, daughter of John and Mary. Born July 19, 1780. p. 171

Smith, Isaac, son of Isaac and Judith. Born May 16 and Baptized June 20,
1762. p. 23

Smith, John, son of Peter and Bathsheba. Born February 8 and Baptized
March 20, 1757. p. 14

Smith, John, son of Thomas and Dorothy. Born May 10, 1759. p. 18

Smith, Judith, daughter of Isaac and Judith. Born November 26, 1760. p.20

Smith, Judith, daughter of Peter and Bathsheba. Born September 2 and
Baptized October 5, 1777. p. 166

Smith, Margaret Briscoe, daughter of James and Elizabeth. Born ____1773
and Baptized July 27, 1773. p. 154

Smith, Mary, daughter of Isaac and Judith. Born March 15, 1758. p. 16

Smith, Mary, daughter of Peter and Bathsheba. Born July 25, 1770. p. 37

Smith, Perrin, son of Peter and Bathsheba. Born February 28, 1768. p.33

Smith, Peter, son of Peter and Bathsheba. Born November 24, 1765. p. 29

Smith, Sally, daughter of Peter and Bathsheba. Born July 29, 1772. p.151

Smith, Sarah, daughter of William and Bathsheba. Born November 28, 1774
and Baptized January 3, 1775. p. 158

Smith, Susannah, daughter of Isaac and Judith. Born March 26 and Baptized
April 13, 1771. p. 39

Smith, Thomas Buckner, son of Elizabeth Smith. Born ____1773 and
Baptized September 11, 1773. p. 154

Smith, Thomas, son of Thomas and Dorothy. Born July 6, ____. p. C

Smith, _____, daughter of Thomas and Dorothy. p. B

Snow, John, son of Cuthbud and Sarah. Born September 20, ____. p. C

Snow, Judith, daughter of Cuttred and Sarah. Born June 12, 1757. p. 15

Snow, Sarah, daughter of Cutbud and Sarah. Born July 16 and Baptized August 19, 1759. p. 18

Snow, William, son of Cuthbert and Jane. Baptized January 8, 1775. p.158

Soaper, James, son of John and Joyce. Born September 14 and Baptized September 18, 1777. p. 166

Soles, Mary, a bastard daughter of Elizabeth Soles. Born February 25, 1766. p. 30

Soper, John, son of William and Mary. Born January 4, 1781. p. 171

Soper, Mary, daughter of William and Mary. Born February 2, 1784. p. 171

Soper, Mildred, daughter of John and Joyce. Born October 26 and Baptized November 3, 1772. p. 152

Soper, Priscilla, daughter of John and Ann. Born May 2 and Baptized May 27, 1759. p. 18

Soper, William, son of John and Joyce. Born November 25, 1774 and Baptized January 1, 1775. p. 158

Soper, William, son of William and Mary. Born May 10, 1794. p. 174

Spencer, Ann, daughter of Robert and Mary. Born May 14 and Baptized June 25, 1774. p. 156

Spencer, Elliot, son of Robert and Sally. Born December 22 and Baptized December 31, 1771. p.40

Spencer, Thomas Hayes, son of Robert and Sally. Born August 19, 1768. p.34

Sprat, James, son of James and Sarah. Born September 16, 1758. p. 16

Sprat, William, son of James and Sarah. Born December 19, 1756 and Baptized January 23, 1757. p. 13

Stedar, Letitia, daughter of Thomas and Susannah. Born July 23 and Baptized August 18, 1771. p. 39

Stedar, Elisabeth, daughter of John and Ann. Born May 18 and Baptized June 15, 1777. p. 165

Stedder, Betsy, daughter of Thomas and Susanna. Born December 24, 1773 and Baptized February 20, 1774. p. 155

Stedder, John, son of James and Elizabeth. Born March 12 and Baptized April 21, 1776. p. 162

Stedder, John, son of John and Ann. Born February 27 and Baptized March 7, 1774. p. 156

Stedder, John, son of Thomas and Susanna. Born October 30 and Baptized December 1, 1776. p. 163

Stevens, Absalom, son of Nathaniel and Elizabeth. Born ____1773 and Baptized April 4, 1773. p. 153

Stevens, Elizabeth, daughter of William and Sarah. Born June 19 and Baptized July 27, 1766. p. 30

Stevens, John, son of William and Elizabeth. Born December 18, 1775 and Baptized January 30, 1776. p. 161

Stevens, Lucy, Baptized June 8, 1777. p. 165

Stevens, Robert, son of Benjamin and Elizabeth. Born June 20, 1766. p.30

Stevens, Tabitha, daughter of Benjamin and Elizabeth. Born January 20 and Baptized March 19, 1769. p. 35

Stewart, John, son of James and Lettitia. Born December 29, 1766 and Baptized February 26, 1767. p. 31

Stewart, William, son of James and Letitia. Born November 20, 1768 and Baptized January 22, 1769. p. 34

Stuart, Armistead, son of James and Letitia. Born September 20 and Baptized November 2, 1777. p. 166

Stuart, Betsy, daughter of James and Letitia. Born April 24 and Baptized June 21, 1772. p. 151

Stuart, Elizabeth Ryland, daughter of John and Margaret. Born January 29 and Baptized March 1, 1772. p. 40

Stuart, James, son of James and Letitia. Born December 24, 1774 and Baptized January 15, 1775. p. 158

Stuart, Mary, daughter of John and Margaret. Born June 7 and Baptized July 16, 1775. p. 160

Stuart, William, son of John and Margaret. Born December 19, 1773 and Baptized January 16, 1774. p. 155

Summers, Betty, daughter of John and Mary. Born March 24 and Baptized
    May 3, 1767. p. 32

Summers, John, son of John and Mary. Born December 17, 1769 and Baptized
    January 21, 1770. p. 36

Summers, John, son of John and Mary. Born July 17 and Baptized August 19,
    1772. p. 151

Summers, William, son of Richard and Betty. Born October 10 and Baptized
    November 5, 1775. p. 160

T

Tabb, Bailey Seaton, son of Robert and Elizabeth. Born August 10, 1762. p. 23

Tabb, Elizabeth, daughter of Robert and Elizabeth. Born June 3, 1759. p. 18

Tabb, Mariana, daughter of John Tabb, Esq. and Frances. Born _____ 1771 and
    Baptized April 7, 1771. p. 39

Tabb, Mary, daughter of Robert and Elizabeth. Born February 20, 1768. p.33

Tabb, Robert, son of Robert and Elizabeth. Born November 29, 1763. p. 26

Tabb, Susanna, daughter of Robert and Elizabeth. Born April 8, 1761. p.21

Tabb, William, son of Robert and Elizabeth. Born January 16, 1766. p.30

Tabor, Judith, daughter of Joseph and Mary. Born August 26 and Baptized
    September 8, 1776. p. 163

Terrell, Margaret, daughter of Michael and Susannah. Born October 10, 1781.
    p. 171

Terrier, Benjamin and Eleanor, twins of John and Eleanor. Born August 26
    and Baptized October 26, 1775. p. 160

Terrier, Mary, daughter of Phillip and Dilly. Born April 3 and Baptized
    May 17, 1776. p. 162

Terrier, Thomas, son of John and Eleanor. Born March 1 and Baptized March 2,
    1772. p. 40

Thomas, Abraham, son of Anthony and Elizabeth. Born January 13 and
    Baptized March 1, 1776. p. 161

Thomas, Ann, daughter of James and Sarah. Born July 17 and Baptized
    August 11, 1776. p. 163

Thomas, Ann, daughter of William and Judith. Born January __, 1776 and
    Baptized March 10, 1776. p. 161

Thomas, Ann Lewis, Sp. daughter of Mary Thomas. Born March 20 and
Baptized May 5, 1776. p. 162

Thomas, Armistead, son of William and Judith. Born February 3 and
Baptized March 3, 1771. p. 38

Thomas, Elizabeth, daughter of Morgan and Elizabeth. Born November 2 and
Baptized December 27, 1767. p. 33

Thomas, Elizabeth, daughter of William and Leah. Born March 16, 1814.
p. 178

Thomas, George, son of Humphry and Ann. Born February 28, 1757. p. 14

Thomas, George Armistead, son of William and Leah. Born July 14, 1808.
p. 177

Thomas, James Davis, son of Mark and Ann. Born August 10, 1792. p. 174

Thomas, James, son of Morgan and Elizabeth. Born November 22, 1763 and
Baptized January 15, 1764. p. 26

Thomas, James, son of William and Judith. Born June 16 and Baptized
July 14, 1765. p. 29

Thomas, Jesse, son of James and Sarah. Born January 13 and Baptized
March 3, 1771. p. 38

Thomas, Joel, son of James and Sarah. Born March 10 and Baptized
May 4, 1766. p. 30

Thomas, John Davis, son of William and Leah. Born May 2, 1812. p. 177

Thomas, Josiah, son of William and Judith. Baptized February 27, 1774.
p. 155

Thomas, Judith, daughter of James and Sarah. Born May 13 and Baptized
June 14, 1768. p. 33

Thomas, Lewis, son of William and Leah. Born December 14, 1802. p. 176

Thomas, Mark, son of James and Sarah. Born March 31 and Baptized
April 8, 1764. p. 27

Thomas, Mary, daughter of James and Sarah. Born January 8 and Baptized
February 20, 1757. p. 14

Thomas, Mary, daughter of William and Leah. Born November 15, 1803. p. 177

Thomas, Matthew, son of James and Sarah. Born June 22 and Baptized
July 22, 1759. p. 18

Thomas, Matthew, son of Morgan and Elizabeth. Born September 15 and Baptized October 24, 1773. p. 154

Thomas, Mildred, daughter of Mark and Mildred. Born February 23 and Baptized March 12, 1775. p. 158

Thomas, Rosyann, daughter of William and Leah. Born March 22, 1816. p. 178

Thomas, Sally, daughter of James and Sarah. Born April 3 and Baptized May 9, 1773. p. 153

Thomas, Sally, daughter of Mark and Mildred. Born February 14 and Baptized March 23, 1777. p. 164

Thomas, Susanna Frances, daughter of William and Leah. Born June 11, 1810 p. 177

Thomas, William Bartlet Foster, son of Mark and Ann Thomas. Born April 18, 1794. p. 174

Thomas, William Boram, Sp. son of Joanna Thomas. Born January 9 and Baptized February 11, 1774. p. 155

Thomas, William, son of William and Judith. Born January 22 and Baptized March 19, 1769. p. 35

Thomas, William Edward, son of William and Leah. Born October 24, 1806. p. 177

Thomas, _____n, son of James and Sarah. Born June 1755 and Baptized July 13, 1755. p. 11

Tomkins, John, son of John and Hannah. Born April __, 1770 and Baptized April 23, 1770. p. 37

Tomlin, John, son of Solomon and Ann. Born April 13 and Baptized May 16, 1777. p. 165

Tomlin, Mary, a bastard daughter of Elizabeth Tomlin. Born July 3 and Baptized August 2, 1772. p. 151

Tomlin, Samuel, son of Samuel Tomlin of Somerset Co., Maryland, and Elizabeth. Born April 6 and Baptized September 21, 1771. p. 39

Tompkins, Elizabeth Kemp, daughter of Robert and Mildred. Born April 15 and Baptized June 13, 1773. p. 154

Tompkins, Elizabeth Simpton, daughter of William and Ann. Born ____, 1772 and Baptized April 26, 1772. p. 40

Tompkins, Mildred, daughter of Robert and Mildred. Born January 23 and Baptized March 28, 1762. p. 22

Toyes, John, son of Henry and Ann Williams. Born July 4 and Baptized August 22, 1756. p. 12

Treacle, Dawson, son of William and Elizabeth. Born February 3 and Baptized March 28, 1762. p. 22

Treacle, John, son of John and Susanna. Born July 12 and Baptized August 15, 1762. p. 23

Treacle, John, son of William and Elizabeth. Born October 23 and Baptized December 11, 1757. p. 15

Treacle, Mary, daughter of William and Elizabeth. Born February 14 and Baptized April 8, 1764. p. 27

Treacle, Susannah, daughter of William and Elizabeth. Born June 6 and Baptized June 27, 1756. p. 12

Treacle, William, son of John and Susanna. Born December 10, 1759 and Baptized February 3, 1760. p. 19

Treacle, William, son of William and Elizabeth. Born October 13 and Baptized November 11, 1759. p. 19

Treakle, Elizabeth, daughter of William and Elizabeth. Born January 20, and Baptized February 23, 1766. p. 30 30

Turner, Ann, daughter of John and Elizabeth. Born March 29 and Baptized April 29, 1759. p. 17

Turner, Cynthia Ann, daughter of William and Elizabeth. Born June 22, 1809. p. 177

Turner, Daniel, son of William and Elizabeth. Born January 25, 1811. p. 177

Turner, Elizabeth, daughter of John and Elizabeth. Born December 6, 1757 and Baptized March 5, 1758. p. 15

Turner, Hester, daughter of George and Ann. Born September 10 and Baptized October 26, 1758. p. 16

Turner, Joyce, son of John and Elizabeth. Born May 20 and Baptized June 22, 1760. p. 20

Turner, Mary, daughter of John and Elizabeth. Born June 25 and Baptized July 25, 1756. p. 12

Turner, Ralph, son of John and Elizabeth. Born February 1 and Baptized March 13, 1763. p. 25

Turner, William, son of George and Ann. p. A

Turner, William, son of John and Elizabeth. Born August 5, 1785. p. 172

Tyrrel, James, son of Michael and Susanna. Born June 25 and Baptized July 30, 1775. p. 160

Tyrrel, Mary, daughter of Michael and Susanna. Born January 24 and Baptized February 27, 1774. p. 155

Tyrrel, Nicholas, son of Michael and Susanna. Born May 16 and Baptized June 15, 1777. p. 165

W

Walden, James, son of Charles and Mary. Born September 4, 1756. p. 13

Walker, Matilda, daughter of George and Mary. Born November 8, 1794. p. 174

Walker, Polley Thurston, daughter of George and Mary. Born April 6, 1792 p. 174

Walker, Robert Dixon, son of George and Mary. Born May 29, 1797. p. 175

Waller, Franky, daughter of Nelson and Dorothy. Born September 11 and Baptized October 3, 1773. p. 154

Ward, Ann Ross, daughter of Thomas and Clare. Born August 17 and Baptized September 29, 1776. p. 163

Ward, Richard Laughlin, son of Thomas and Clare. Born April 13 and Baptized May 15, 1774. p.156

Waters, Mary, daughter of Francis and Elizabeth. Born June 17 and Baptized July 22, 1759. p. 18

Watson, Machen Jervis, son of _____ and Lydia Watson. Baptized November 28, 1773. p. 155

Watson, Mary, daughter of John and Hannah. Born March 10 and Baptized April 6, 1777. p. 164

Wedmore, John, son of Edmond and Sarah. Born December 4, 1763 and Baptized February 12, 1764. p. 26

Welch, James Anderton, a bastard child of Margaret Welch. Born April 1, 1756. p. 12

Weston, Betsey, daughter of Major and Frances. Born July 1 and Baptized August 15, 1762. p. 23

Weston, Degge, son of Robert and Lettitia. Born May 8 and Baptized
June 24, 1759. p. 18

Weston, Dolly, daughter of Major and Frances. Born July 23 and Baptized
August 26, 1764. p. 27

Weston, Franky, daughter of Major and Frances. Born November 24, 1769 and
Baptized February 18, 1770. p. 36

Weston, George, son of Major and Frances. Born November 11 and Baptized
December 12, 1756. p. 13

Weston, Jenny Stuart, daughter of John and Judith. Born May 27, 1770. p.37

Weston, Judith, daughter of John and Judith. Born May 28 and Baptized
July 1, 1764. p. 27

Weston, Mary, daughter of John and Judith. Born April 14 and Baptized
May 17, 1767. p. 32

Weston, Mary, daughter of Major and Frances. Born August 11, ____. p. C

Weston, Nanny, daughter of John and Judith. Born April 5, 1759. p. 17

Weston, Nanny, daughter of Major and Frances. Born October 12 and
Baptized November 12, 1758. p. 17

Weston, Robert, son of Major and Frances. Born July 31 and Baptized
September 7, 1766. p. 31

Weston, Salley, daughter of John and Judith. Born March __, 1761 and
Baptized April 26, 1761. p. 21

Weston, William, son of John and Judith. Born April 16 and Baptized
May 9, 1773. p. 153

Weymouth, John Davis, son of Mary Weymouth. Baptized November 12, 1775.
p. 160

White, Absalom, son of Absalom and Frances. Born September 3, 1811. p.177

White, Absalom, son of William and Dorothy. Born October 29 and
Baptized December 14, 1777. p. 166

White, Anna, daughter of James and Ann. Born May __, 1775 and Baptized
June 18, 1775. p. 159

White, Ann Elizabeth, daughter of John and Ann. Baptized July 7, 1776.
p. 162

White, Ann Davis, daughter of William and Elizabeth. Born June 13 and
Baptized August 9, 1767. p.32

White, Arthur Bennet, son of John A. and Martha W. Born January 10, 1823.
p. 178

White, Bartlet, son of Edward and Pembroke. Born October 14, 1788. p. 173

White, Cary Washington, son of Bartlet and Paulina. Born August 1, 18__.
p. 178

White, Cyrina Wesley, daughter of Bartlet and Paulina. Born January 21,
1820. p. 178

White, Cyrus Cary, son of Absalom and Frances. Born June 30, 1819. p. 178

White, Cyrus James, son of Bartlet and Paulina. Born November 4, 18__. p.178

White, Dudley, son of Edward and Pembroke. Born September 30, 1780. p. 171

White, Edward, son of Absalom and Frances. Born _____, 1813. p. 177

White, Edward, son of Edward and Pembroke. Born July 24, 1784. p. 172

White, Edward Chisley, son of Joseph and Miriam. Born June 19, 1820 and
Died August 15, 1840. p. 178

White, Elizabeth James, daughter of Absalom and Frances. Born November 8,
1815. p. 178

White, Elizabeth, daughter of Edward and Pembroke. Born May 25, 1779. p.171

White, Elizabeth, daughter of Thomas and Elizabeth. Born November 15, 1790.
p. 173

White, Elizabeth, daughter of William and Elizabeth. Born September 23 and
Baptized November 9, 1760. p. 20

White, Elizabeth Lee, daughter of William and Dorothy. Born November 29,
1786. p. 172

White, Emery Ann Eliza, daughter of Joseph and Miriam. Born August 31,
1822. p. 178

White, Frances, daughter of William and Dorothy. Born November 16, 1779.
p. 171

White, George Washington, son of Absalom and Frances. Born February 22,
1823. p. 180

White, George, son of John and Joyce. Born October 29 and Baptized
December 5, 1773. p. 155

White, George, son of Richard and Mary. Born July 25 and Baptized
September 20, 1767. p. 32

White, Harriet Frances, daughter of Absalom and Frances. Born October 6, 1817. p. 178

White, Henrietta Frances, daughter of Joseph and Miriam. Born July 14, 1826 and departed this life 11 August 1827. p. 180

White, Henry, son of Edward and Pembroke. Born October 15, 1782. p. 171

White, Hilligan Diggs, daughter of Absalom and Frances. Born March 3, 1821. p. 178

White, Isaac, son of William and Dorothy. Born September 16, 1792. p.174

White, James, son of James and Annah. Born May 18 and Baptized June 22, 1760. p. 20

White, James, son of John and Joyce. Born October 20, 1765 and Baptized January 12, 1766. p. 29

White, James Cary, son of Joseph and Miriam. Born April 5, 1818. p. 178

White, James, son of Richard and Mary. Born May 18 and Baptized June 12, 1757. p. 14

White, Jesse, son of John and Joyce. Born December 16, 1770 and Baptized January 20, 1771. p. 38

White, John Callis, son of John and Joyce. Born January 8 and Baptized February 21, 1768. p. 33

White, John, son of William and Elizabeth. Born February 27, 1758. p. 16

White, Joseph Davis, son of Edward and Pembroke. Born October 6, 1792. p. 174

White, Mary, daughter of Edward and Pembroke. Born September 13, 1786. p. 172

White, Mary, daughter of James and Annah. Born July 23 and Baptized October 9, 1763. p. 25

White, Mary, daughter of John and Mary. Born May 20 and Baptized June 20, 1762. p. 23

White, Mary, daughter of Richard and Mary. Born July 7 and Baptized July 19, 1770. p. 37

White, Mary, daughter of William and Elisabeth. Born July 21 and Baptized August 2, 1755. p. 11

White, Nancy, daughter of Edward and Pembroke. Born November 1, 1796. p. 175

White, Nancy, daughter of Richard and _____. Born December 26, 1764 and Baptized January 16, 1765. p. 28

White, Nanny, daughter of James and Annah. Born June 25 and Baptized August 10, 1766. p. 30

White, Richard, son of James and Annah. Born October 24 and Baptized December 11, 1757. p. 15

White, Richard, son of Richard and Mary. Born May 30 and Baptized July 4, 1762. p. 23

White, Robert, son of James and Anna. Born November 22 and Baptized December 22, 1771. p. 40

White, Robert Throckmorton, son of John and Ann. Born November __, 1772 and Baptized December 3, 1772. p. 152

White, Rosey, daughter of William and Dorothy. Born October 30, 1790. p. 173

White, Salley, daughter of Richard and Mary. Born May 18 and Baptized June 24, 1759. p. 18

White, Samuel Davis, son of Thomas and Elizabeth. Born August 20, 1785. p. 172

White, Sarah, daughter of William and Elizabeth. Born March 25 and Baptized April 24, 1763. p. 25

White, Thomas Bartlet, son of Bartlet and Paulina. Born July 4, 1818. p.178

White, Thomas Degge James, son of Absalom and Frances. Born October 26, 1809. p. 177

White, Thomas, son of Thomas and Elizabeth. Born May 1, 1787. p. 172

White, Thomas, son of William and Dorothy. Born July 31, 1781. p. 171

White, Wesley Franklin, son of Absalom and Frances. Born September 7, 1826 p. 180

White, William Henry, son of Bartlet and Paulina. Born May 24, 1816. p. 178

White, William Kitson, son of Edward and Pembroke. Born February 18, 1800. p. 176

White, William, son of James and Annah. Born March 29 and Baptized April 16, 1769. p. 35

White, William, son of Richard and Mary. Born March 29 and Baptized May 9, 1773. p. 153

White, William, son of William and Dorothy. Born September 20, 1794. p.174

White, William, son of William and Elizabeth. p. A

White, _____, daughter of John and Mary. p. B

Whiting, Judith, daughter of Matthew and _____. Born February __, 1770 and Baptized March 28, 1770. p. 36

Whiting, Harriet, daughter of Henry and Humy Frances (Humphry Frances Toye - see marriages page 22). Born April 7 and Baptized May 18, 1771. p. 39

Wiatt, _____, daughter of Benjamin and Margaret. Baptized April 1755. p. D

Wiley, Elizabeth Edwards, daughter of William and Sarah. Baptized October 5, 1777. p. 166

Williams, Abraham Iveson, son of Daniel and Frances. Born April 1, 1771. p. 39

Williams, George, son of Daniel and Frances. Born January 21 and Baptized February 20, 1757. p. 14

Williams, Joanna, daughter of Thomas and Martha. Born January 16 and Baptized February 17, 1760. p. 19

Williams, John, son of William and Abbigail. Born June 22 and Baptized October 9, 1763. p. 25

Williams, Nancy Ballard, daughter of William and Abigail. Born January 18 and Baptized May 10, 1772. p. 40

Williams, Patty, daughter of Thomas and Martha. Born August 14 and Baptized November 13, 1757. p. 15

Williams, Peggy, daughter of Samuel and Margaret. Baptized January 9, 1776. p. 161

Williams, Rice, son of John and Sarah. Born January 23, 1759. p. 17

Williams, Thomas, son of Daniel and Francis. Born April 2 and Baptized May 15, 1768. p. 33

Williams, Thomas, son of Francis and Elizabeth. Born August 31 and Baptized October 5, 1777. p. 166

Williams, Thomas, son of Thomas and Martha. Born April 25 and Baptized May 19, 1765. p. 28

Williams, William, son of Daniel and Frances. Born February 12, 1765. p. 28

Williams, William, son of John and Sarah. Born August 19, 1755. p. 11

Williams, _____, daughter of Thomas and Martha. Baptized February 9, 1755. p. D

Willis, Ann, daughter of John and Mary. Born August 6 and Baptized September 10, 1775. p. 160

Willis, Augustine, son of John and Mary. Born November 30, 1773 and Baptized January 27, 1774. p. 155

Willis, Elizabeth, daughter of John and Jane. Baptized June 16, 1771. p. 151

Willis, George, son of George and Ann. Born June 17 and Baptized July 13, 1755. p. 11

Willis, George, son of John and Jane. Born October 6 and Baptized November 28, 1756. p. 13

Willis, James, a bastard son of Elisabeth Willis. Born July 12 and Baptized August 24, 1755. p. 11

Willis, James, son of James and Sarah. Born June 21, 1757. p. 15

Willis, John, son of John and Mary. Born July 28 and Baptized August 24, 1777. p. 165

Willis, John, son of William and Ann. Born August 2 and Baptized August 25, 1776. p. 163

Willis, Mary, daughter of William and Mary (?). Born September 29 and Baptized October 24, 1773. p. 154

Willis, Mildred, daughter of John and Mary. Born May 5 and Baptized June 21, 1772. p. 151

Willis, Molly, daughter of James and Hannah. Born May 1, 1767. p. 32

Willis, Molly, daughter of John and Jane. Born July 28 and Baptized August 29, 1762. p. 23

Willis, Nancy, daughter of John and Jane. Born March 14 and Baptized May 11, 1760. p. 19

Willis, Patty, daughter of John and Jane. Born March 4 and Baptized April 2, 1769. p. 35

Willis, Richard, son of Henry and Ann. Baptized September 3, 1774. p. 157

Willis, Salley, daughter of John and Jane. Born December 10, 1757 and Baptized January 22, 1758. p. 15

Willis, Thomas, son of John and Mary. Born February 21 and Baptized
   March 12, 1776. p. 162

Willis, William, son of John and Mary. Born April 14 and Baptized
   May 27, 1770. p. 37

Willis, William, son of Thomas and Ann. Born September 19, 1756. p. 13

Willis, _____, son of Thomas and _____. Baptized 1755. p. D

Wilson, James, son of John and Caty. Born June 14 and Baptized June 30,
   1776. p. 162

Winder, Mary, daughter of Thomas and Elisabeth. Born July 13 and
   Baptized July 27, 1755. p. 11

Window, Edmond, son of John and Ann. Born September 4 and Baptized
   October 17, 1756. p. 13

Window, Elizabeth, daughter of Thomas and Elizabeth. Born January 28,
   1759. p. 17

Window, James, son of John and Ann. Born January 23 and Baptized
   March 29, 1771. p. 38

Window, Molley, daughter of John and Ann. Born June 26, 1760. p. 20

Wren, John, son of Kilbe and Elizabeth. Born July 16 and Baptized
   August 11, 1765. p. 29

Wright, Mary, daughter of William and Priscilla. Baptized August 13,
   1775. p. 160

Wright, Susannah, daughter of William and Priscilla. Born April 1 and
   Baptized April 12, 1772. p. 40

★ ★ ★

The last name of the father was not legible on the following births:

_____, Joice Degge, daughter of Joshua and Johannah. Born
   November 29, 1788. p. 172

_____, Daniel Carmines, son of Daniel and Elizabeth. Born
   May 2, 1802. p. 176

_____, William, son of Edward and Margaret. Born October 23,
   1756 and Baptized November 14, 1756. p. 13

_____, Julian, daughter of Gabriel and Betsy. Born January 25,
   1803. p. 176

DEATHS

B

Baker, Charles, died February 1, 1752. p. 105

Baker, Elizabeth, died February 8, 1758. p. 106

Bell, Mary, died December 17, 1771. p. 109

Billups, John, died November 5, 1759, son of Robert Billups, p. 107

Billups, Langley, died August 4, 1771. p. 109

Billups, Richard, died February 2, 1752. p. 105

Blacknall, Mrs. Ann, died September 24, 1758. p. 107

Brokes, Thomas, died January 28, 1757. p. 106

Brown, Ralph, died March __, 1772. p. 110

Burton, Charles, died before June 27, 1777, husband of Ann. p. 165 (see page 35 births)

Burton, _____, son of William Burton died October 26, 1759. p. 107

C

Christian, Israel, died April 7, 1752, son of Israel. p. 105

Christian, John, died June 21, 1756. p. 106

Curtis, Charles, died November 4, 1759. p. 107

D

Davis, Edward, died November 6, 1759. p. 107

Davis, Elizabeth, died June 7, 1770. p. 109

Davis, James, died about November 16, 1758, son of James and Alice Davis. (see page 41 births)

Davis, John, died February 3, 1781, Clerk of this Parish. p. 110

Davis, Leah, died about February 19, 1757, daughter of James and Alice Davis. (see births page 42)

Davis, Thomas, died November 25, 1751, son of John and Dorothy Davis. p.105

Dawson, Thomas, died July 28, 1770, Clerk of the new Church. p. 109

Debdnam, Charles, died November 12, 1759. p. 107

Degge, Isaac, died November 9, 1759, son of Augustine Degge. p. 107

Degge, Joshua, died October 31, 1759, son of Augustine Degge. p. 107

Degge, William, died November 22, 1754. p. 105

Dixon, The Rev. John, professor of Divinity at the College and sometime Rector of this Parish was buried May 9, 1777 in the new Church.
p. 110

Dudley, William, died January 15, 1760. p. 108

E

Eddens, Lucy, died January 8, 1757. p. 106

Eddens, Thomas, died November 5, 1759. p. 107

Elliott, Seaton, died January 29, 1758. p. 106

F

Flippin, Sarah, died May 18, 1772. p. 110

Fordam, Edward, died February 22, 1754. p. 105

Forrest, William, died December 2, 1759, son of George Forrest. p. 108

Foster, Sarah, died October 20, 1760, daughter of John and Rose. p. 108

Frood, Frederick John (alias Stevens) died May 8, 1772. p. 110

G

Gayle, Christopher, died October 8, 1771. p. 109

Gayle, Joyce, died January 22, 1752. p. 105

Gayle, Joseph, died _____ 1771. p. 109

Gwyn, John, died September 12, 1770, drowned in Milford Haven, son of Humphry Gwyn. p. 109

Gwyn, Lucy, died March 16, 1771, daughter of Humphry. p. 109

H

Harris, Alice, died August 16, 1754. p. 105

Hayes, Dorothy, died July 25, 1751, wife of William Hayes. p. 105

Hayes, James, died September 9, 1754. p. 105

Hayes, Thomas, died August 17, 1751, son of James Hayes. p. 105

Hayes, James, died March 26, 1750, son of William and Dorothy Hayes. p. 103

Hayes, Captain William Hayes died June 6, 1771. p. 109

Hays, Dorothy, died May 15, 1770, wife of Captain Thomas Hays. p. 109

Hays, Captain Thomas Hays died May 29, 1770, husband of Dorothy. p. 109

Hudgen, William, died October 12, 1771. p. 109

Hudgin, William, died before December 22, 1772, husband of Dorothy Hudgin. (see births page 66)

Hundley, Martha, died May 15, 1757. p. 106

Hunley, Elizabeth, died December 21, 1751. p. 105

Hunley, Joshua, died December 16, 1751. p. 105

Hunley, Philip, Sr., died September 12, 1770 aged 85 years. p. 109

Hunley, Philip, died September 12, 1770. p. 109

Hunley, Sarah, died November 14, 1759. p. 107

Huntley, Esther, died May 11, 1772. p. 110

Huntley, Lucy, died March 2_, 1772 p. 110

Huntley, Robert, died May 2_, 1772. p. 110

Huntley, Wilkinson, died May __, 1772. p.110

I

Iveson, Richard, died January 6, 1760. p. 108

Iveson, Thomas, died December 31, 1759. p. 108

J

Jarret, Dorothy, died October 17, 1759. p. 107

Jarret, Jane, died March 29, 1772. p. 110

Jarvis, Francis, died May 24, 1772. p. 110

Jervis, Mary, died January 1750, wife of John Jervis. p. 105

Jones, George W. born December 26, 1791 and died July 15, 1793, son
 of Charles and Lettitia Jones. p. 173 (see births page 76)

Jones, Mary, died November 16, 1759. p. 107

K

Keys, Ann, died January 2, 1772. p. 110

Knight, Rebecca, died December 14, 1754. p. 105

L

Lewis, Thomas, died November 3, 1759, son of Thomas. p. 107

Longest, Ann, died January 4, 1772, wife of William Longest. p. 110

Longest, Elizabeth, died November 6, 1759. p. 107

Longest, William, died January 2, 1772, husband of Ann. p. 110

Longest, Winifred, died March 2_, 1772. p. 110

M

Machen, Richard, died December 12, 1770. p. 109

Machen, Captain Thomas, died December 22, 1759. p. 108

Marchant, Richard, died February 26, 1772. p. 110

Merchant, Abraham, died May 10, 1751. p. 105

Miller, Franciss, died April 6, 1754. p. 105

Morgan, Judith, died November 13, 1758. p. 107

Morgan, Mary, died January 4, 1760. p. 108

Mullins, George, died February 13, 1772. p. 110

N

Nason, John, died May 10, 1772. p. 110

Neithercut, Margaret, died February 2, 1751. p. 105

Newell, Elizabeth, died October 16, 1758. p. 107

Newell, Mary, died November 18, 1758. p. 107

O

Owen, Moses, died January 11, 1759. p. 107

P

Peed, Elias, died January 10, 1760. p. 108

Plummer, John, died October 4, 1759, son of C. William. p. 107

Plummer, Mary, died April 26, 1752. p. 105

Pugh, Mary, died February 28, 1753. p. 105

R

Ransone, Lettitia, died January 11, 1760. p. 108

Reade, Lucy, died July 15, 1772. p. 110

Reade, Mary, died November 6, 1759, daughter of C. Gwyn. p. 107

Reade, Robert, died October 26, 1759, son of Robert Reade. p. 107

Redman, Jeremiah, died May 28, 1770. p. 109

Respess, John, died April __, 1772. p. 110

Ripley, Ann, died November 21, 1751. p. 105

S

Sadler, Benjamin, died April 29, 1754. p. 105

Sampson, Thomas, died before August 20, 1773, husband of Joyce. (see births, page 99)

Samson, Mary, died July 3, 1758. p. 106

Singleton, Anthony, died February 19, 1752. p. 105

Smith, Ann, died January 5, 1752. p. 105

Smith, Perin, died January 30, 1752. p. 105

Soper, James, died August 21, 1757. p. 106

Spencer, Sarah, died December 27, 1771. p. 109

Stevens, Frederick John (alias Frood), died May 8, 1772. p. 110

Stevens, Sarah, died March 2, 1772. p. 110

Summers, Lucy, died January 20, 1760. p. 108

T

Thomas, Humphry, died January 27, 1758. p. 106

Todd, Mary, died November 18, 1758. p. 107

Tompkins, Peter, died July 13, 1770, son of William Tompkins. p. 109

W

Weston, Robert, died September 15, 1750. p. 103

White, Edward Chisley, born June 19, 1820 and died August 15, 1840, son of Joseph and Miriam White. p. 178 (see births page 110)

White, Henrietta Frances, born July 14, 1826 and died August 11, 1827, daughter of Joseph and Miriam. p. 180 (see births page 111)

White, James, died November 9, 1759, son of James. p. 107

Williams, Johannah, died November 15, 1753, daughter of Daniel and Frances Williams. p. 105

Willis, Ann, died October 14, 1759. p. 107

Wooden, Sarah, died May 13, 1757. p. 106

INDEX

Adams,
    Ann   24
    Elizabeth   15
    James   1
    Mary   24
    Nancy   24
    Stephen   24
    Zechariah   1,24

Alleman,
    John   1

Alman, (See Almun)
    Mary   9

Almun (See Alman)
    Letitia   12

Amiss, (See Amys)
    Ann   24
    Lucy   24
    William   24

Amys, (See Amiss)
    William   1

Anderson,
    Edward   1,24
    Frances   24
    Francess   24
    John   1,24
    William   24

Anderton,
    Benjamin   24
    Dicky   24
    Dorothy   24
    Elizabeth   24
    George   24
    Isaac   24
    Jane   24,25
    John   24,25
    Joseph   25
    Mark   1,24,25
    Mary   24,25
    Mildred   25
    Ralph   25
    Richard   25
    Sarah Hunley   25
    Thomas   25

Anderton, Cont'd
    William   1,24,25

Angel,
    Benoni   1
    Elizabeth   2
    Jemmy   25
    John   25
    Josiah   25
    Marget   25
    Mary   14,25
    Robert   25
    William   25

Armistead,
    Ann   25,26
    Anna   25
    Anna Cleve   25
    Betty   26
    Catharine   25
    Caty   25,26
    Currel   1,26
    Dorothy Reade   26
    Elizabeth   25,26
    Francis   1,26
    George   1,26
    Harkey   1
    John   1,25,26
    Judith   21
    Judith Carter   26
    Lucy   26
    Margaret   26
    Mary   5,25,26
    Mary (Mrs.)   18
    Mildred   26
    Ralph   26
    Rebecca   6
    Richard   1,25,26
    Robert   25,26
    Sarah   26
    Susanna   26
    William   25,26
    _____   1

Ashbury,
    Joseph   1

Assetin,
    David (Dr.)   26
    Elizabeth   26

Atherton,		Barnet, (See Barnett) Cont'd	
Charles	2	Frances	27
		Mary Marlow	27
Ayers, (See Ayres)		William	27
Ann	21		
		Barnett, (See Barnet)	
Ayres,		James	27
Ann	13	Johanna(h)	27
James	26	William	27
Joanna	26		
John	2,26	Barton,	
Mary	12	John	2

B

		Baset,	
		Dolly	27
Bagas,		Dorothy	27
Jane	19	Elizabeth Hunley	27
		Jesse	27
Bagwell,		John	27
Samuel	2	Judith	28
		Mary	1,27,28
Baillie, (See Baley, Bayley)		Rachel	27,28
Robert	2	Richard	27
		Thomas	28
Baker,		William	2,27,28
Ann Elizabeth	26		
Charles	116	Baster,	
Elizabeth	116	John	2
John	26		
Sarah	26	Baxter,	
Sarah (Mrs.)	8	Elizabeth	28
		James	28
Baley, (See Baillie, Bayley)		John	28
Elizabeth	26	Mary	13,28
John	26		
Matthew	2,26	Bayley, (See Baillie, Baley)	
Robert	26	Elizabeth	28
William	26	Mary	28
		Robert	28
Banks,			
Ann	19,27	Beard,	
Ann Smither	26	Ann	3,28
Elizabeth	26,27	Dorothy	28
Isaac	27	Elizabeth	23
James	26,27	John	2,28
J<u>e</u>mmy	27	Joice	19
John	2,27	William Hudgen	28
Joshua	27		
Josiah	27	Be<u>h</u>tley,	
Joyce	4,27	Mary	28
Mary	19	Richard	28
Mildred	6	William	28
Milly	27		
Barnet (See Barnett)		Belfore,	
Dorothy	27	Elizabeth	8

Bell,
    Elizabeth   28
    Mary   116
    Peter   2,28

Bernard,
    Frances   14
    Henry   28
    James   28
    Mary   18,28
    Peter   2
    Robert   2

Biggs,
    Mary   12

Billups,
    Ann   4,14,28,29,116
    Anna   8
    Christopher   28
    Elizabeth   7,28,29
    Elizabeth Cary   29
    Frances   29
    George   29
    Hugh Gwyn   29
    Humphry   29
    Humpry   2
    John   2,28,29,116
    Joseph   29
    Joyce   29
    Langley   29,116
    Letitia   7
    Lucy   29
    Mary   7,28,29
    Mildred   29
    Richard   116
    Robert   2,28,29,116
    Rosanna   29
    Sarah   21,29
    Sarah (Mrs.)   23
    Sarah Gwyn   29
    Sukey   9
    Susanna   29
    Thomas   2,29
    Thomas Elliott   29

Bird,
    Frances   20
    (Sir) John Peyton   20

Blacknall,
    Ann   9,116
    Betty   11
    Charles   30
    Fanny   30

Blacknall - Cont'd
    Frances   2
    Mary   15,30
    Mary (Mrs.)   3
    Richard   30
    Sarah   16

Blake,
    Ann   30
    Dorothy   30
    Elizabeth   30
    James   2,30
    Jonathan   2
    Mary   30
    Mildred   30
    Robert   30
    Sarah   30
    William   2,3,30

Bloxham,
    John   30
    Sarah   30

Blunt,
    Bartholomew   3

Bohanan, (See Bohannon, Bohonnan)
    Mary   30
    Sarah Jordan   30
    William   3,30

Bohannon (See Bohanan, Bohonnan)
    Elizabeth   5
    Esther   30
    Hester   2
    Judith   30
    Mary   30
    Nanny   30
    William   30

Bohonnan (See Bohanan, Bohannon)
    Joseph   30
    Mary   30
    William   30

Bond,
    Anna   30
    Fanny   30
    William   30

Boram, (See Borum)
    Benjamin   30
    Edmond   30
    Edmund   30,31
    Edward   3,31

Boram, - Cont'd			Bridge - Cont'd	
Frances	30,31		Elizabeth	31
Franky	30		John	3,31
Joanna	31		Joshuah	3
John	3,31		Mary	31,92
Mary	15,31		Polly	31
Nancy	31		Ransom	31
Sally Jean	31		Robert	31
Susannah	9		William	3,31
William Thornton	31			
			Bridges,	
Borum, (See Boram)			Elizabeth	32
Edmond	31		Frances	32
Elizabeth Scott	31		John	32
Thomas Scott	31		Mildred	32,52
			Richard	3,32
Borten,			Sally Edwards	32
Mary	13		Susannah	3
Boss,			Bristo, (See Bristow)	
Hayes	31		Henry	3
John	31			
Joseph	3,31		Bristow, (See Bristo)	
Nanny	31		Mary	32
Sarah	31		Robert	32
Susannah	31		Samuel	32
Boswell,			Brokes,	
Elizabeth	23,31		Thomas	116
Jane	31			
John	31		Bromley,	
Lucretia	31		Augustin	3
Mary	31		Robert	3
Panranparabo	3,31		Sarah	4
Robert	3,31			
Sarah	31		Bromly,	
Sukey	31		Milly	11
Susanna	31			
Thomas	31		Brommel,	
			Peter	3
Bramham, (See Branham)				
Mary	31		Brookes, (See Brooks)	
Richard	3,31		Dorothy	8
Sarah	31		George	32
			Johannah	19
Branham, (See Bramham)			John	32
Richard	3,31		Joyce Keeble	32
Sally	31		Mary	14,32
			Nancy	32
Breedlove,			Susanna(h)	32
Judith	16		Thomas	32
			William	32
Bridge,			Brooks, (See Brookes)	
Ann	16,31		Ann	6

Brooks, (See Brookes)- Cont'd
    Ann Smith   32
    George   3
    Joseph   3
    Richard   32
    Thomas   3

Brounley, (See Brownley, Brownly, Brounly)
    Abigail   33
    Ann   15,32
    Archibald   3,32,33
    Augustine   33
    Betty   33
    Catherine   16
    Edward   32,33
    Elizabeth   32,33
    Foster   33
    Frankey   33
    George   33
    James   3,33
    Jesse   33
    John   33
    Judith   33
    Lucy   33
    Margaret   33
    Mary   33
    Robert   33
    Sally   32
    Sarah   3,32,33
    Thomas   3,33
    William   4,32,33

Brounly, (See Brounley, Brownley, Brownly)
    Ann   33
    Archibald   4
    Mildred   12
    Sarah   33
    William   33

Brown,
    Ann   34
    Anna   8
    Christopher   4
    Dorothy   18,34
    Francis   4,34
    George   4,34
    Jane   12
    Jemmy Gayle   34
    Judith   16,34
    Judith Longest   34
    Mary   13,34
    Ralph   116

Brown, - Cont'd
    Richard Gayle   34
    Robert   4,34
    William   4,34

Brownley (See Brounley, Brounly, Brownly)
    Abigail   34
    Ann   34
    Archibald   34
    Augustine   34
    Betty   34
    Caty   34
    Dorothy   34
    Edward   35
    Elizabeth   34,35
    Frances   34
    James   34,35
    Jesse   34
    Joannah   35
    John   34
    Lucy   35
    Margaret   34,35
    Martha   35
    Mary   34
    Milley   35
    Priscilla   35
    Robert   34,35
    Sarah   34,35
    Thomas   34
    William   34,35

Brownly (See Brounley, Brownley, Brounly)
    William   4

Brumley,
    Edward   4
    William   4

Buchannan,
    Elizabeth   17

Buckner,
    Elizabeth   35
    Mary   35
    Mordicia   4
    Thomas William   4
    William   35

Bum,
    Alice   35
    Salley   35
    Thomas   35

Burge,
    Joyce 35
    Mary 35
    William 4,35

Burges, (See Burgess)
    Davis 35
    Elizabeth 35
    John 35
    Mary 35
    Mary Alexander 35
    Willoughby 35

Burgess, (See Burges)
    John 4,35

Burton,
    Ann 35,116
    Charles 4,35,116
    Elizabeth 12,35,116
    John 35
    Mary Charles 35
    Mildred 35,36
    Nancy 36
    William 35,116

Bush,
    Dorothy Longest 36
    George 4,36
    Macy 36
    Richard 4
    Sarah 15

C

Calles,(See Callice, Callis, Callys)
    Mary 8

Callice, (See Calles, Callis, Callys)
    Elizabeth 36
    Richard 36
    Robert 36

Callis, (See Calles, Callice, Callys)
    Ambrose 4,36,37
    Ann 36,37
    Elizabeth 10,36,37
    Frankey 36
    Franky 16
    Gabriel 36
    George 36

Callis, (See Calles, Callice, Callys) -Cont'd
    James 36,37
    John 36
    Joice 22
    Lewis 36
    Mary 12,36,37
    Molly 36
    Nancy 7
    Nanny 37
    Richard 4,37
    Robert 36,37
    Sally 37
    Susanna 20,36,37
    William 36,37

Callys, (See Calles, Callice Callis)
    Jos_____ 4

Camp,
    Mary 37
    Robert 37
    Thomas 4,37

Campbel,
    Alexander 37
    Nanny 37
    Susanna 37

Carey, (See Cary)
    Dudley 37
    John 5
    Lucy 37

Carmines,
    Daniel 37
    Elvira Frances 37
    Hilligan 37

Carney,
    Ann 37
    Elizabeth West 37
    Mary 11
    William 5,37

Carter,
    George 5,37
    James 5,37
    Jane 37
    Mary Edloe 37
    Rebecca 37
    William 37

Cary, (See Carey)			Clerk, (See Clark)	
Ann	21		Elisabeth	38
Dorothy	14,37		Richard	38
Dudley	5		Thomas	38
Elizabeth	37			
John	37		Coad,	
Margaret (Mrs.)	21		Hannah	38
Mary	8		Mary	38
			Michael	38
Chamberlain,				
Ann	8		Coleman, (See Colman)	
			Ann	87
Chandler,				
Elly	37		Collins,	
Joyce	37		John	5
Lucy	37			
William	37		Colman, (See Coleman)	
			Ann	87
Chapman,				
Henry	5		Colvin,	
			William	5
Charley,				
Elizabeth	37		Cook,	
Frances	37		Mordicai	5
Robert	37			
			Cooke,	
Chase,			Averilla	38
John	5		Ignatius	5,38
			Mildred	38
Christian,				
Bailey	37		Corbin,	
Elizabeth	13		Ann Lee	38
George	37		Annah	38
George Reade	37		Gawin	38
Israel	37,38,116		Jane Byrd	38
John	38,116		Susannah	38
Letitia	37		William	38
Martha	6,37,38			
			Cosby,	
Clare,			James	5
Elizabeth	38			
Frances	38		Cowper,	
John	38		Abraham	5
Clark, (See Clerk)			Coye,	
Elizabeth	38		Charles M.	5
Joseph	38			
Richard	5,38		Crauley, (See Crawley)	
Thomas	38		Abraham	38
William	38		Dorothy	38
			Thomas	38
Cleaver,				
Judith	8		Crawford,	
			Elizabeth	22

Crawley, (See Crauley)		Curtis,	
Abraham	5,38	Ann	18
Ann	16	Bridget	39
Elizabeth	38	Catherine	39
William	38	Charles	39,116
		Christopher	5
Cray,		Edmund	39
Alexander	39	James	40
Ann	38	John	39,40
Elizabeth	22,38,39	Mary (Mrs.)	7
James	38,39	Sarah	39,40

D

Cray, (continued)
- John 5,38
- Judith 38
- Mary 15,38,39
- Mary James 38
- Mildred 38,39
- Milley 39
- Richard 5
- Sarah 38
- William 39

Dagnall,
- Sarah 13

Dale,
- John 5

Dance,
- James 40

Creadle, (See Creedle)
- Benjamin 39
- Elizabeth 39

Darricot,
- William 5

Creedle, (See Creadle)
- Benjamin 39
- Betsey 39
- Elizabeth 39
- William 39

Davis,
- Alice 40,41,42,43,116,117
- Ann 6,19,40,41,43
- Armistead 40
- Betty 40
- Billups Hudgin 40

Culley, (See Cully)
- Christopher 39
- Elizabeth Dudley 39
- George 39
- George A. 39
- Henry Loyd 39
- John L. 39
- Judith 39
- Julian 39
- Mary 39
- Ralph 5,39
-   5

Davis, (continued)
- Catharine (Catherine) 40,41,42
- Christopher 40,41,42
- Daniel 40
- Dickey 40
- Dolly 40
- Dorothy 22,40,41,42,43,117
- Edward 6,40,41,42,43,116
- Elizabeth 6,13,18,21, 40,41,43,116
- Elizabeth Burges 41
- Elizabeth Degge 41
- Elizabeth H. 41,42
- Frances 6,41
- Francis 41,43
- Hillegant 40
- Hillegen 40
- Hillegon 43
- Humphry 6,41
- Isaac 6,40,41,43
- James 6,40,41,42,43,116,117
- James Hudgin 41
- James Marshall 41
- John 6,40,41,42,43,116,117

Cully, (See Culley)
- Ann 39
- Christopher 39
- Elizabeth 39
- Judith 39
- Mary 39
- Robert 39
- Thomas 39

Cuningham,
- Mary 5

(8)

Davis, Cont'd
    Joseph   6,40,41,42,43
    Joyce   6,19
    Leah   42,117
    Letitia Wren   42
    Lettice   40,43
    Lucrecia   43
    Lucretia   40,41,42
    Lucy   13,42
    Martha Ann Jackson   42
    Mary   4,15,17,40,41,42,116
    Meredith   42
    Mildred   21
    Nancy   42
    Nancy Bailey   42
    Paulina Frances   42
    Philip   42
    Ralph Armistead   42
    Rebecca   40
    Sally   42
    Sarah   6,8,9,12,19
          40,41,42,43
    Stephen   41
    Sukey   3
    Susanna   1,3,9,42
    Thomas   6,40,41,42,43,117
    William   43
    ____ard   6
    _____   23

Dawson,
    Ann   15,43,44
    Christopher   6
    Elizabeth   2,43
    James   6,43,44
    John   6
    Leonard   43,44
    Mary   11,43,44
    Mary Booker   44
    Robert Hudgin   44
    Samuel   43,44
    Thomas   44,117
    William Holder   44

Deal,
    James   6
    John   44

Dean,
    Josiah   44
    Rosanna   44
    Rosanna Lilly   44

Debdnam,
    Charles   117

Debnam, (See Debdnam)
    Elizabeth   21

Deforrest,
    Cornelius   6

Degge,
    Ann   44,45
    Anthony   44,45,46
    Augustine   44,45,46,117
    Avarilla   44
    Averilla   16,45,46
    Bailey   44
    Bathsheba   44
    Betty   44,45,46
    Caty   44,46
    Charles   44
    Christopher   44
    David   44
    Elizabeth   6,8,23,45
    Henry   45
    Isaac   45,117
    James   45
    Jesse   45
    Joel   45
    Johannah   11
    John   6,45
    Joseph   44,45,46
    Joshua   44,45,46,117
    Joshuah   6,44
    Josiah   45,46
    Joyce   45
    Lauson   45
    Lawson   45
    Louisa   45
    Mary   9,20,44,45,46
    Molly   46
    Rebecca   46
    Sarah   44,45,46
    Simon   46
    William   6,44,45,46,117

Delaney,
    Edward   6

Dennis,
    Elizabeth   46
    Elizabeth Davis   46
    James   46
    William   46

Dickson,
    Lucretia   1

Digges,
    Mary   46

Digges, Cont'd
    Nancy   46
    William   46

Dixon,
    Ann   46
    Elizabeth   13,46
    John   6,46,117
    John, Jr.   46
    John (Rev.)   46
    Joyce   20
    Lucretia   46
    Lucy   46
    Susanna   46
    Thomas (Capt.)   6,46
    Tindsly   46
    William   7,46

Dobson,
    Robert   7

Dowdy,
    Lawrence   7

Driver,
    Mary   46
    Richard   46
    Susanna   46
    William   46

Ducket,
    Elizabeth   22

Dudley,
    Ann   47
    Ann Billups   47
    Anna   5
    Armistead   47
    Charles   47
    Dorothy   5
    Frances   2
    George   7
    George Alexander   7,47
    Jane   5
    John   7
    Judith   7
    Martha   14
    Mary   13,47
    Rebecca   47
    Robert Ballard   47
    Sally   47
    Sarah   7
    Thomas   7
    William   7,47,117
    William Todd   7

Dunbar,
    Elizabeth   12

Dunlavy,
    Ann   47
    Anthony   47
    Mary   47
    William   47

Dunla__
    William   7

Duplecy,
    Amy   47
    Betsy   47
    Charles   47
    Sarah   47

DuPlese,
    Charles   7

Dye,
    Richard   7,47
    Suky   47

E

Eddens,
    Ann   47
    Dawson   7,47
    Elizabeth   2,47
    John   7,47
    Langley Billups   47
    Letitia   47
    Lucy   47,117
    Nancy   47
    Samuel   7,47
    Sarah   47
    Susannah   47
    Thomas   47,117
    Thomas Cary   47

Edmundson,
    Robert   7

Edwards,
    Ann Whiting   10
    Betty   15
    Charles   7
    Thomas Whiting   7

Elliot,
    Anna   7
    Dorothy   5
    Frankey   15

Elliot, Cont'd		Fitchet, (See Fichet(t), Fittchet)	
Jane	5	Ann	48
Mary	11	Joshua	48
Rhoda	19	Salathiel	48
William	7	Sarah	48
		Susanna	48
Eliott,		Thomas	8,48
Ann	22	William	48
Seaton	117		
William	8	Fitchett,	
		Ann	23
Ellis,			
Catherine	48	Fittchet,	
Robert Evans	48	Daniel	48
		Sarah	48
Emerson,			
John	48	Fitzhugh,	
Mary	48	George	8
Peggy	48		
		Fitzsimmons,	
Enos,		Anna	16
Francis	8,48		
Robert	48	Fletcher,	
Sarah	48	John	8
Sary	48	Thomas	8
William	48		
		Flippen, (See Flippin)	
Evans,		Armistead	49
Anna	48	Dorothy	49
Betsey	48	Humphry	48
Franky	48	Jenny	49
George	48	Sarah	48
John	8	Thomas	48,49
Judith	48		
Lannas	48	Flippin (See Flippen)	
Lewis	8,48	Dorothy	2,49
William	8,48	Elizabeth	18
		Humphry	8,49
F		John	49
		Machen	49
Fercharson,		Mary	49
Philip	8	Nancy Davis	49
		Sarah	117
Fichet, (See Fitchet(t))		Susanah	17
Daniel	48	Thomas	8,49
Sarah	48		
William	48	Flucher,	
		Ann	49
Filyoung,		John	49
Elizabeth	48	Thomas	49
George	8,23,48		
		Fordam, (See Fordham, Fordom and Foredom)	
Finch,			
Catherine	5	Edward	117

(11)

Fordam, (See Fordham, Fordom and
          Foredom) Cont'd
    Hannah   5
    Mary   20

Fordham,
    Elizabeth   13

Fordom,
    Edward   49
    Elizabeth   49
    Judith   15
    Margaret   49

Foredom,
    Hannah   22

Forrest,
    Abraham   8
    Alice   49
    Ann   49,50,51
    Anna   49,50
    Betsy   49
    Dorothy   49,50
    Dorothy Elliott   49
    Edmond   8
    Edmund   49
    Elizabeth   16,49,50
    Elizabeth Hunley   49
    Frances   21
    George   8,49,50,51,117
    Henry   8,49,50
    James   50
    Jesse   50
    John   8,49,50,51
    Joyce   50
    Letitia Hayes   50
    Mary   8,9,49,50,51
    Matthew   50
    Molly   50
    Nancy   50
    Philip   8,50,51
    Richard   50
    Sally   51
    Sarah   51
    Susanna   18,21
    Thomas   50,51
    William   117

Forster, (See Foster)
    Bathsheba   20
    Isaac   8

Foster, (See Forster)
    Alice   51

Foster, (See Forster) Cont'd
    Amelia   51
    Ann   51,53
    Anne   11
    Bathsheba   20
    Betsey   51
    Betty   10,51
    Betty Jordan   4,53
    Caty   51,52,53
    Christopher   9,52
    Elizabeth   51,52,53
    Francis   9,51
    George   9,51
    Isaac   52,53
    James   51
    Jesse   51
    Jesse Johnson   51
    Joel   9,51,52,53
    John   51,52,53,117
    Joseph   52
    Joshua(h)   9,51,52,53
    Josiah   9,51,52,53
    Judith   52,53
    Louisa   11,52
    Mary   22,51,52,53
    Nanny   53
    Peter   9,53
    R._____   52
    Richard   51,53
    Robert   9,51,52,53
    Rose   51,52,53,117
    Rosey   53
    Sally   53
    Sarah   9,21,53,117
    Susanna(h)   21,51,53
    Susanna Ransone   53
    Thomas   9
    William   9,53
    _____   9

Fowler,
    Ann   53
    John   9,53
    Lucy Lilly   53

Frood, (See Stevens)
    Frederick John   117

G

Gale, (See Gayle)
    Elizabeth   53
    Margaret   20
    Matthew   53
    Susannah   53

Gayle, (See Gale)
    Ambrose 53
    Ann 4,54,55
    Anne 6
    Betsey 54
    Billups 54
    Caty 9,54
    Christopher 54,55,117
    Dorothy 4
    Elizabeth 9,14
    Elly 54
    Frances Bernard 17
    George 9,54,55,56
    Hannah 18,54,55,56
    Hunley 9
    James 9
    Joanna 54
    John 9,54,55
    John Edwards 54
    Joseph 9,54,55,117
    Josiah 53,54,55
    Joyce 12,54,117
    Judith 9
    Leah 54
    Levin 54
    Lucretia 54
    Lucy 9,18,55
    Lucy Jones 55
    Margaret 55
    Mary 6,53,54,55
    Mathew 9,54,55
    Matthew 9,54,55,56
    Matthews 54
    Matthias 54,55,56
    Robert 9,54,55
    Sarah 9,13,54,55
    Susanna(h) 9,54,55,56
    Thomas 9,54,56
    _____ce 9

Gibbons,
    Ann 56
    Charles Blacknall 56
    Mary 56
    Nancy 56
    William 9,56

Gibson,
    Mary 56
    Robert 56
    Sarah (Mrs.) 2

Giles,
    Ann 56
    John 56

Glascock,(See Glasscock)
    Abraham 56
    Ann 9
    Dorothy Hayes 56
    Elizabeth 56
    Isaac 10
    John 56
    Mary 56
    Richard 56

Glasgow,
    Ann 56
    Elizabeth 56
    Isaac 56

Glasscock,(See Glascock)
    Abraham 10,56
    Ann 56
    Ann Whiting 56
    Elizabeth 56
    Isaac 56
    John 10,56
    Mary 56
    Richard 56
    Robert 56
    William 56

Godfrey,
    Ann 56
    Eley Burd 56
    John 56
    Louisa Jackson 56

Going (See Gowing)
    Ann 57
    Joseph 57
    Priscilla 57
    Sarah 3

Gordon,
    John 10
    Mary 3

Gowing, (See Going)
    Joyce 22
    Lucy 13
    Priscilla 23

Graves,
    John 10

Green,
    Ann 57,58
    Anna 57,58
    Anne 19

Green, Cont'd			Gwyn, Cont'd	
Betsy	57		Walter	10
Caleb Hunley	57		William	59
Caty	57,58		**H**	
Christopher	57			
Elizabeth	14,57,58		Hackney,	
George	10,57,58		Ann	59
James	10,57,58		Jacob	59
James Gowing	57		James Jones	59
James Hunley	57			
Jenny	57		Hall,	
John	10,57,58		Ann	9,59,60
Joseph	58		Betty Jordan	9
Martha Wescom	58		Edmond	10
Mary	22,57,58		Jenny	1
Nancy	58		Joyce	59
Rachel	58		Nanny	59
Richard	57,58		Robert	59,60
Robert	10,57,58		Spence	60
Sally	57,58		Susannah	16
Samuel	57			
Sarah	12,57,58		Hankins,	
Simon	57,58		Sarah	6
Susanna(h)	57,58			
William	10,57,58		Hardisty,	
			Edward	10
Grigs,				
George	59		Harper, (See Harpur)	
Margaret	59		Elizabeth	60
Susannah	59		James	10,60
			Mary	60
Grisset,			Susanna	60
James	10			
			Harpur, (See Harper)	
Guess,			Averilla	60
————	21		James	60
			Mary	60
Gwyn,				
Ann	10		Harris,	
Daniel	59		Alice	118
Dorothy	59		Anthony	10,60
Elizabeth	59		Betty James	60
Elizabeth Toye	59		Dorothy	60
Frances	59		Elizabeth	23,60
Francis	59		Henry	60
Harry	59		James	10,60
Humphry	10,59,117		Jane	13
John	10,59,117		Jesse	60
Letitia Hayes	59		Joanna	60
Lucy	59,117		Johanna	2,60
Martha Peyton	59		John	60
Mary Tabb	59		Mary	60
Mildred	59		Matthias	60
Robert	10		Parthenia	12
Thomas Peyton	59		Rose	60

Harris, Cont'd
   Sarah   60
   William   10

Harrow,
   Mary Moore   60
   Sarah Ann   60
   Thomas   60

Hartswell,
   James   10

Hayes, (See Hays)
   Betty   60
   Dorothy   118
   Dorothy Gwyn   60
   Elizabeth   60,61
   Hugh   10,61
   Hugh Elliott   61
   James   118
   John   60,61
   John Plummer   61
   John Tabb   61
   Margaret   17
   Martha   11,61
   Mary   5
   Mary Hardin   61
   Mildred Smith   61
   Mordecai Cook   61
   Sally   20
   Sarah   61
   Thomas   61,118
   Thomas, Jr.   11
   William   61,118
   William (Capt.)   118
   ————   11

Hays, (See Hayes)
   Dorothy   118
   Thomas (Capt.)   118

Haywood,
   Elkin (Elakin)   11,61
   Elizabeth   61
   John   61

Hensley,
   Jane   61
   Joseph   61
   Polly   61

Hewel, (See Hewil, Huell)
   Judy   61
   Sarah   61
   Thomas   11

Hewel(l) Cont'd
   William   11,61
   William Smither   61

Hewil, (See Hewel, Huell)
   Thomas   11

Hill,
   Ann   1,61
   Catharine   18
   Elizabeth   10
   Salley (Sally)   7,61
   Susanna   13
   Thomas   61

Hilling,
   Lucy   61
   Thomas   61
   William   11,61
   William Candy   61

Hobdy,
   Brookes   11,61
   John   61
   Mary   61

Hodges,
   Ann   62
   Benjamin   62
   Charles   62
   Elizabeth   8,13,14,18,62
   James   62
   Letitia   1
   Mary   14,62
   Richard   11,62
   Samuel   62
   Sarah   62

Holder,
   Frances   1

Hudgen, (See Hudgin, Hudgins)
   Aaron   62,63
   Alban   64
   Ambrose   65
   Ann   2,62,63,64,65
   Annah   66
   Anthony   62
   Archibald   62
   Averilla(h)   5,62
   Basshe (Bathsheba)   62
   Caty   62
   Christopher   62
   Dolly   62
   Dorothy   62,63,64,66

Hudgen, Cont'd
- Edward(s) 62
- Elizabeth 62,63,64,65
- Emmanuel 63
- Fanny 63
- Frances 63,64,65,66
- Gabriel 62,63,64,65
- George 62,63
- Hillegin 62
- Holder 63
- Hugh 11,63
- Humphry 63,64
- Isaac 63
- James 62,63,64
- Jenny 65
- Jesse 63
- Joana 63
- Joann 63
- Joanna(h) 62,63,64,65,66
- John 62,63,64,65
- Joshua 64,65
- Joshua Degge 64
- Joyce 62,63,64,65
- Judith 64
- Kemp 64
- Lewis 11,62,63,64,65
- Lucretia 63,64
- Mary 62,63,64,65
- Mildred 63,65
- Milley (Milly) 65
- Molly 65
- Moses 63,65
- Nancy 65
- Perrin 63
- Rebecca 63,64
- Robert 65,66
- Sarah 62,63,64,65,66
- Susanna Sanford 65
- Sukey (Suky) 62,63,65
- William 62,63,64,65,66,118
- William Holder 66

Hudgin, (See Hudgen, Hudgins)
- Alban 11,66
- Ambrose 11
- Amelia 66
- Ann 15,16,66,67
- Ann Jarvis 66
- Ann Willis 66
- Anthony 66,67,68
- Archibald 66
- Betty 66
- Beverley 66
- Catharine 67,68

Hudgin, (Cont'd
- Caty 11
- Diggs 66
- Dilly 20
- Dorothy 2,17,66,118
- Elizabeth 3,4,7,10,15,66,67,68
- Frances 66,67
- Gabriel 11,66
- Holder 11,66
- Hugh 67
- Humphry 11,66,67
- Hunley 66
- Isaac 67
- Iveson 67
- James 11,66,67
- Joanna 66
- John 11,66,67,68
- John Wilson 67
- Joshuah 11
- Joice 66
- Joyce 66
- Kemp 66
- Kemp Whiting 11
- Lewis 66
- Louisa 67
- Lucretia 11
- Lucyna 67
- Mary 3,6,66,67
- Maryan 67
- Moses 11,66,68
- Nancy 67
- Perrin 11
- Peter 67
- Polly (Polley) 67
- Robert 67
- Rose 67
- Sally 17,66,67,68
- Sarah 4,67,68
- Suky (Sukey) 66,67
- Thomas 67
- Wescom 67
- William 11,12,66,67,68,118
- ———— 12

Hudging,
- Elizabeth 21

Hudgins, (See Hudgin, Hudgen)
- Aaron 12
- Amelia 68
- Ann 5,68
- Betsy 68
- Betsy Soper 68

(16)

Hudgins, Cont'd	
Elizabeth	14,68
Gideon Washington	68
John	68
John Foster	68
Mary Degge	68
Robert	12
Rosanna	68
William	68

Huell, (See Hewel, Hewil)

Milly	68
Sarah	68
William	68

Hugate, (See Hugget)

Alice	68
Ann	68
James	68

Huggart,

James	12

Hugget, (See Hugate)

Dolly	68
Elizabeth	68
James	68

Hughes,

Ann	68,69
Edward	68,69
Elizabeth	68,69
Elizabeth Jones	68
Francis	68
Gabriel	68,69
Harriet	68
Hugh	68
John	68
Lux	68
Richard	69
Robert	69
Susanna(h)	69
Susanna Throckmorton	69
Thomas	69
William	69

Hundley, (See Hunley, Hunly, Huntley)

Ann	69
Elisabeth	69
Henry	69
James	69
John	69
Joyce	69

Hundley, Cont'd	
Judith	69
Lettitia	69
Martha	118
Mary	69
Matthew	69
Nanny	69
Richard	69
Sarah	69
Thomas	69

Hunley, (See Hundley, Huntley)

Ambrose	71
Ann	14,20,69,71
Anna	10
Anthony	69
Caleb	12,70,71
Cathrine	10
Dorothy	69
Elizabeth	3,10,12,69 70,71,118
Frankey	70
George	70
Henry	69,70,71
Humphry	70
James	12,70
James Harris	70
Jane	13,70
Jeriah	70
John	12,70,71
John Biggs	70
Joshua	12,118
Joyce	22,69,70,71
Joyce Smith	70
Lettitia	70,71
Mary	1,8,11,69,70,71
Matthew	70,71
Matthias	12,69,70
Nancy	71
Nanny	71
Nehemiah	69,71
Parthenia	70,71
Philip	12,71,118
Priscilla	17
Ransone	69,70
Richard	12,70,71
Robert	12,70,71
Rose	69,71
Rose (Mrs.)	6
Sarah	5,23,70,71,118
Susannah	14
Sary	70
Susanna(h)	71
Thomas	12,69,70,71

Hunley, Cont'd		
Wilkinson	12,69,71	
William	12,70,71	

Hunly, (See Hundley, Hunley, Huntley)
Elizabeth	71
Letitia	19,71
William	71

Huntley, (See Hundley, Hunley)
Esther	118
Henry	12
Lucy	118
Matthew	12
Robert	118
Wilkinson	118

Hurst,
Betsy	71
Edward	13
Elizabeth	4,71,72
Frances	71
Jesse	71
John	13,71,72
Mildred	71,72
Richard	71,72
Sarah	72
William	72

I

Iveson,
Abraham	13,72
Ann	14
Fanny	72
Jane	8
Mary	72
Richard	118
Susanah	4
Thomas	118

J

Jackman,
John	72
Mary	72
William	72

Jackson, (See Jacson)
Anna	72
George	13,72
John	72
Mary	72
Thomas	13
William	13,72

Jacson, (See Jackson)
George	72
John	72
Judith	72
Mary	72
Betsey	72,73
Betty	10,73

James,
Cary	72
Catherine	72
Cyrum Cooper	72
Cyrus	74
Cyrus B.	72,73
Cyrus Basey	72
Edward	72
Elizabeth	72,73
Elizabeth Hunley	73
Frances	73
Harriot Smith	73
Hilligan Degge	73
John	73
Martha Washington	73
Mary	72,73,74
Matthias	13,72,73
Miriam Marshall	73
Paulina	73
Richard	73
Sarah	73,74
Susanna	73
Thomas	72,73
Thomas Degge Davis	73
Thomas Edward	73
Walter	13,73,74
William	74
William Leven	73

Jarratt, (See Jarret, Jarrot)
Mary	10
William	13

Jarret,
Ann	74
Dorothy	118
George	74
Jane	118
John	74
Thomas	13
William	74

Jarrett,
Anna(h)	74
Betty	74
Elizabeth	74
Thomas	74

Jarrot, (See Jarratt, Jarret)	
John	13
Sarah	19
Jarvice, (See Jarvis)	
William	13
Jarvis,	
Ann	11
Betty	74
Dorothy	10
Edward	74
Elizabeth	3,12,74
Francis	74,119
James	13
John	13
Judith	5
Lindsey	13
Lucy	74
Mary	18
Rose	12
Sally	7
Sarah	13
William	74
Jerrel,	
William	13
Jervis,	
Ann	74,75
Bannister	74
Betty	74
Elizabeth	1,74,75
Francis	13,74,75
Garvin	74
James	74
John	74,75,119
John Dixon	75
Lindsey	75
Lucy	74,75
Mary	5,74,75,119
Patty Read	75
Sally	74
Sarah	75
Thomas	75
Thomas William	75
William	74,75
Johnson,	
Elizabeth	15,75
Frankey	75
Hannah	22
Hugh	13,75
Jane	75
John	13,75

Johnson, Cont'd	
Judith	75
Mary	12,75
Patty	75
Polly Flipping	75
Thomas	13
Johnston,	
John	14
Jones,	
Ann	75,76
Charles	75,76,119
Dorothy	75
Dorothy Cary	75
Edward	75
Edward Simmonds	14
Elizabeth Callis	75
Frances	76
George	76
George W.	76,119
Hannah	16
James	14,75,76
James R.	76
James W.	76
Joyce	76
Letitia, Lettitia	75,76,119
Martha	19
Martha H.	76
Mary	119
Mary Muscow	7
Robert	76
Sally	76
Thomas	14,75,76
William	14

K

Karr,	
Andrew	14
Keeble,	
Elizabeth	76
Lucy	76
Walter	76
	16
Kees, (See Keys, Keyes)	
Ann	76
Catherine	76
Damaris	76
Edward	76
Howard	76
Jean	18
John	76
Lucy	76

Kees, Cont'd			Knight, Cont'd	
Sarah	20		Joseph	77
Sally	76		Mary	77
————	76		Nancy	22
			Rebecca	119
Kemp,			Richard	14,77
Elizabeth	76		Sarah	78
Gregory	76			
William	14,76		Knightman,	
			Elizabeth	78
Keyes, (See Kees, Keys)			Henry	78
Frankey	3		Samuel Thompson	78
Keys, (See Kees, Keyes)			**L**	
Ann	22,76,77,119			
Betty	76		Lambeth,	
Caty	76		Merideth	14
Edward	14,76			
Hillegan	76		Landom,	
Howard	14,76,77		William	14
John	76			
Mary	8,76		Lane,	
Robert	76,77		Mary	78
Salley, Sally	77		Sarah	12
Sarah	3,76,77		Susanna Street	78
Killigrew,			Layton,	
Frances Murry	3		Elizabeth	78
			Reuben	78
King,				
Alexander	77		Lewis,	
Ann	77		Caty	78
Elizabeth	77		Christopher	14,78
James	77		Elizabeth	2,19,78
John	14,77		George	78
Joseph	77		Johanna(h)	21,78
Mary	11,17,77		John	14,78
Mary Ann	77		Lucretia	6,78
Nanny	77		Mary	19,78
Snelling	77		Nancy	78
Thomas	14,77		Nanny	78
			Robert	14,78
Kinnun,			Thomas	14,78,119
Aristarcus	77		————	78
Elizabeth	77			
			Lichfield,	
Knight,			Elizabeth	78
Betsy	77		Francis	78
Elizabeth	77,78		Hezekiah	78
Gabriel	77		John	78
Henry	14,77,78			
Humphry	77		Lilley, (See Lilly)	
Henry	14,77		Mary	2
John	77			

Lilly, (See Lilley)
   Ann   9,79
   Elizabeth   20
   John   79
   Lucy   79
   Mildred   2
   Richard   79
   Rosanna   6
   Thomas   79
   William   79
   William Armistead   79
   ─────────   79

Little,
   Caty   79
   Elizabeth   79
   John   14,79
   Mary   79
   Susanna   79

Longest,
   Ann   79,80,119
   Caleb   79
   Clare   21
   Dorothy   79
   Elizabeth   2,79,119
   Frankey   79
   James   79
   John Jones   79
   Joshua(h)   15,79
   Joshua Floyd   79
   Judith   4
   Lucy   17
   Mary   2
   Mildred   79
   Nancy   79
   Richard   79,80
   Robert Ross   80
   Sarah   8
   Thomas   15,79,80
   William   80,119
   Winifred   8,119
   ─────────   80

Lovel,
   Mary   80
   Richard   80
   Sarah   80

Lowry,
   William   15

Lucas,
   Elizabeth   7

Lucas, Cont'd
   Joyce   18
   Judith   8,13
   Mary   80
   Mary Blacknall   80
   William   15,80

Lunsford,
   Hiriam L.   80
   Sarah L.   80
   Thomas L.   80

Lyell (See Lyle)
   Jonathan   15

Lyle,
   James   80
   John   15,80
   Mary   80

Mc

McCoy, (See Mecoy)
   Charles   80
   Daniel   80
   George   80
   Joanna(h)   80
   Joseph   80

McDougal - MacDougal,
   Daniel   15,80
   Elizabeth   80
   James   80
   John   80

M

Machen, (See Macken)
   Ann   3,80,81
   Averilla   80
   Dorothy   2
   Elizabeth   80
   Frances   3
   John   15,80,81
   Judith   81
   Lettitia   81
   Mary   80,81
   Nancy   81
   Nanny   80,81
   Patty   81
   Peggy   81
   Richard   81,119
   Robert   80,81
   Sally   81

Machen, Cont'd			Matthews, Cont'd	
Samuel	15,80,81		Robert	82
Sarah	80,81		Mayo,	
Susannah	81		John	15
Thomas	81		Joseph	15
Thomas (Capt.)	119		Mecoy, (See McCoy)	
William	80,81		Charles	82
_____ny	81		Francis	82
Macken,			Johannah	82
Lucy	4		Meggs, (See Maggs, Megs)	
Maggs, (See Meggs, Megs)			John	15,82
Thomas	15		Sarah	82
Manuel,			Megs,	
Elizabeth	81		Jenny	82
Milly	81		John	82
Marchant, (See Merchant)			Nancy	82
Abraham	82		Sarah	82
Ann	81,82		Thomas	82
Charlotte	82		Merchant, (See Marchant)	
Christopher	82		Abraham	83,119
Edmund	82		Ambrose	83
Elisha	82		Ann	83
Elizabeth	30,82		Daniel	15
Esther	81,82		Easter	15
Frances	1		Edmond	1,15,83
John	81		Elisha	15
Joyce	82		Elizabeth	7,83
Mary	82		Elizabeth Adams	83
Richard	82,119		Hester	6
Richard Bartlet	82		Johannah	20
Sarah	8		John	83
William Fordham	82		Joyce	83
Mason,			Lucretia	18
Elizabeth	12,82		Lucy	83
Mary	82		Mary	10
Sarah	3		Richard	,15,83
Thomas	15,82		Sarah	83
Massenburgh,			William	15,83
Robert	15		Michael - Michel,	
Masters,			Ann	83
Mary	4		Edward	83
Matthews,			John	83
Ann	82		Joyce	83
Dorothy	15		Judith	83
John Edwards	82		Michen,	
Nancy Thornton	82		Margaret	1

(22)

Millar, (See Miller)		Minter, Cont'd	
Elizabeth	14	Thomas	85
Thomas	15	William	16,85
Miller,		Mintor, (See Minter)	
Alice	9	James	16
Anderson	84	John	16
Ann	6,16,17,83,84,85	Mary	16
Averilla	83,84		
Avy	83	Mitchel, (See Mitchell)	
Betsy	83,84,85	Cyrum	85
Betty	83	Edmond	16
Booker	83	James	85
Catherine	17,83	James C.	85
Caty	83	Mordecai	85
Dorothy	84	Sarah S.	85
Elizabeth	84		16
Ferdelia	83		
Francis	16,83,84,119	Mitchell,	
Franky	84	Edward	86
Gabriel	83,84,85	Johannah	86
Isaac	15,84	Joyce	86
James	15,84		
Jenny Dudley	84	Mongomery, (See Montgommery)	
Joanna	84	David	16
John	83,84		
Joseph	83,84,85	Montgommery,	
Judith	9,83,84	Ann	86
Martha	84	David	86
Mary	4,83,84,85	Leroy	86
Nancy	84		
Nanny	84	Morgan,	
Polly	84	Ann	5,86,87
Rebecca (Rebekah)	3,84	Benjamin	86,87
Roseannah	84	Betsy	86
Sarah	83,84,85	Betty	86
Sally	85	Elizabeth	7,9,19,17,86,87
Seth Foster	85	Forrest	86
Whitney	85	Frances	12
		Franky	86
Minter, (See Mintor)		George	86
Ann	85	James	16,86,87
Anne	85	Jane	13
Anthony	16,85	John	86,87
Elizabeth	4	John Howard	86
Francis	85	Joshua	86
James	85	Judith	86,119
Johannah	17	Mark	16,86
John	85	Mary	12,13,86,87,119
Joice	16	Nancy	86
Josiah	85	Nanny	86
Joyce	11,85	Richard	16,86,87
Judith	85	Sarah	87
Mary	2,85	Suky	87
Sarah			

Morgan, Cont'd			Norris, Cont'd	
Thomas	87		Thomas	88
William	16,86,87			
	87		Nottingham,	
			Esther	88
Morris,			Richard	88
Ann	87		Sarah	88
Elizabeth	87			
James	16		Nuthall, (See Nuttall)	
John	16,87		Sarah	11
Lucy	87			
Mary	87		Nuttall,	
Thomas	87		John	16
William	87			

<u>O</u>

Mullikin,			Oliver,	
Katy	87		Armistead	88
			Graveley (Gravely)	16,88
Mullins,			Judith	88
Elizabeth	3		Sarah	88
George	119			
James	16		Over,	
Mary	4		Elizabeth	88
			John Powel	88

<u>N</u>

Nason,			Owen,	
John	16,119		Ann	88,89
			Anna Boss	88
Neale,			Armistead Lewis	88
Thomas	16		Betsy	88
			Betty	88
Neithercut,			Christopher	88
Margaret	119		Dorothy	88
			Edmond	16,88,89
Newburn,			Edmund	88
Jimmy	87		Elizabeth	88,89
Joyce	87		Frankey	88
Mary	87		George	88,89
Michael	87		Joanna(h)	88,89
Thomas	87		John	89
Thomas Foster	87		Joyce	89
			Joyce Forrest	89
Newel, (See Newell)			Lucrecia	88
John	88		Lucretia	88
Sarah	88		Mary	89
William	88		Molly	89
			Moses	120
Newell, (See Newel)			Nanny	89
Elizabeth	119		Sally	88
Mary	120		Sarah	17,89,96
			Susanna(h)	89
Norris,			Thomas Forrest	89
Elizabeth	88		William	16,88,89
Joseph	88			89

(24)

Pallister,			Peak, (See Peake, Peek)	
Ann	17		Annah	90
John	17,89		Dorothy	90
Mary	89		Elizabeth	90
Mildred	5		Lydia	90
			Robert	90
Palmer,			Susanna	17
Gwyn Read	89		Thomas	90
Lucy	1,89		William	90
Nathaniel	17,89			
			Peake,	
Paris,			Thomas	17
Elisha	17			
			Peck,	
Parrot,			Ann	12
Augustine	89			
Elizabeth	90		Peed, (See Pead, Peade)	
John	17,89		Ann	90,91,92
Joseph	17,90		Caty	14
Machen	90		Dolly	91
Michael	17		Dorothy	91
Richard	17,90		Elias	91,120
Robert	17,90		Elizabeth	16,91,92
Sarah	89		George	91,92
Susanna	90		Humphry	91
			Hundley	91
Parsons,			James	90,91,92
Absalom	90		John	91,92
Bathsheba	90		Joseph	91
Betty	90		Lewis	92
Caty	90		Margaret	17
James	17,90		Mary	91,92
John	90		Milley	91
Judith	90		Nancy	92
Mary	90		Patty	92
Sally	90		Peggy	92
			Philip	17,91,92
Pead, (See Peed)			Priscilla	90,91,92
Fanny Cymer	90		Richard	92
Hundley	90		Robert Hunley	92
Hunley	90		Sarah	92
James	90		Uriah	92
Mary	90		William	91,92
				91
Peade,			Peek, (See Peak, Peake)	
Ann	14,90		Lucy	11
George	90			
James	17,90		Perkins,	
John	90		Whitney	17
Lewis	17,90			
Mary	90		Perrot, (See Parrot, Perrott)	
Sally	90		Elizabeth	92
Susanna	90		Fanny	92
Thomas	17,90			

Perrot, Cont'd			Pleacy,	
	George	17,92,93	Caty	18
	George Nevil	92	Joice	20
	James	92		
	Joanna	92	Plummer,	
	John	17,92	George	17,93
	Lucy	92,93	Johannah	5
	Mary	7	John	120
	Richard	92,93	Judith	18,93
	Robert	92,93	Kemp	93
	Sarah	92	Margaret	93
	Susanna	92	Mary	120
			Thomas	93
Perrott,				
	Elizabeth	2	Pointer,	
			Henry	17
Peterson,			Seth	17
	Alice	93		
	Caty	93	Pool, (See Poole)	
	Mary	93	Robert	18,94
	Peter	17,93	Susannah	94
Pew,			Poole, (See Pool)	
	Ann	93	Elizabeth	14
	Elizabeth	2	Thomas	18
	Johanna(h)	93		
	Josiah	93	Powel, (See Powell)	
	Mary	93	Betty	94
	Sarah	93	Edmond	94
	William	17,93	Elizabeth	94
		93	Henry	94
			Joanna	94
Peyton,			John	94
	Elizabeth	6,93	Mary	94
	Frances	10,93	Mildred	94
	Francis (Frances)	93	Rosannah	94
	Harriet	21	Sarah	23
	Harriot	93		
	Henry Yelverton	93	Powell, (See Powel)	
	(Sir) John	93	Henry	94
	Martha	22	John	18,94
	Martha Cook	93	Mary	94
	Mary	20,21,93	William	94
	Seignora	93		
			Powers,	
Pied, (See Pead, Peed)			John	94
	James	17	Salley	94
			Sarah	94
Pigot,				
	Galen	17	Presley, (See Pressley)	
			John	94
Pilot,			Mary	94
	Rose	2	William	94
Plater,			Pressley, (See Presley)	
	Ann	20	John	18

Price,	
Thomas, the Rev. Mr.	18
Pritchard,	
Hannah	94
Henry	94
John	18,94
Joyce	94
Mildred	10
Robert	94
William Lucas	94
Pritchet,	
Joseph	18
Pugh,	
Elias	18,94
Mary	120
Susanna	94
William Forrest	94
Purcell,	
Elizabeth	94
James	94
Purnall,	
John	18
Pursley,	
Mary	6
Putman,	
Dorothy	5
Sukey	7
Susannah	10

Q

Quin,	
Elizabeth White	94
Mary	17,94
Peter	18,94
Sally	94
Sarah	94

R

Ransom,	
Richard	18
Ranson, (See Ransone)	
James	95
Lettitia	95
Ransone,	
Ann	2,10,95

Ransone, Cont'd	
Augustine	18
Dorothy	10
James	95
Lettitia	95,120
Lucy	95
Matthew James	95
Richard	95
Robert	95
Sarah	95
Read, (See Reade)	
Dorothy	95
Gwyn	95
John	18
Mary	95
Reade, (See Read)	
Dorothy	1,10,95
Dorothy Clock	95
Gwyn	18,95
James	18,95
John	95
Judith	95
Judith Armistead	95
Lucy	17,120
Mary	120
Robert	120
Sarah	95
William	95
Reaves,	
Robert	18
Redman,	
Jeremiah	120
Mary	16
Repress, (See Respes, Respess)	
Lucy	95
Richard	95,96
Respes,	
Ann	11
Elizabeth	10
Richard	18
Susanah	18
Thomas	18
Respess, (See Repress, Respess)	
Ann	95
Elizabeth	95,96
Elliot	95
John	95,120

Respess,			Robins, Cont'd	
Judith	16		Anna(h)	96,97
Lucy	95,96		Anner	97
Machen	95		Betsy	96
Mary	96		Edmond Lewis	96,97
Matthew	96		Edmund	96,97
Richard	96		Elizabeth	96,97,98
Robert	95,96		George William	96
Susanna	95		James	96,97
Thomas	95,96		Joanna	97
			John	96,97
Reynolds,			Judith	96,97
Catherine	96		Letitia	97
Dorothy	96		Lucretia	97
John	18,96		Mary	96,97,98
Sally	96		Milly	97
William	18,96		Nancy	97
William Younger	96		Nancy Soper	97
			Peter	96,97,98
Rice,			Polly	97
Amy	7		Robert	97
Catherine	23		Sarah	97
Elizabeth	21		Susanna	97
Sarah	22		Thomas	97
			William	19,96,97,98
Ripley, (See Riply)				
Ann	1,120		Robinson,	
Deborah	96		Henry	19
Fanny	96		John (Major)	98
John	96		Mary	98
Judith	96		Peter	98
Lucy	96			
Mary	96		Rogers,	
Philip	96		Ann	98
Richard	96		John	19
Thomas	96		Mary	98
William	96		Thomas	19,98
Riply, (See Ripley)			Royston,	
Andrew	96		Robert	19
Deborah	96			
John	96		Ruff,	
			Ann	98
Robbins, (See Robins)			John	98
Alban	19		Sally	98
Peter	19			
Williams	19		R_____	
			Margaret	98
Roberts,			Robert	98
Elizabeth	17			
			S	
Robins, (See Robbins)			Sadler,	
Alban	96,97,98		Ann	14,98,99
Ann	96,97			

Sadler, Cont'd			Shackelford, Cont'd	
Averilla	98		Charles	99
Benjamin	120		Maria	99
Betty	20,98		Martha	99
Edward	98		Shipley,	
Henry Atherton	98		Ann	99
Jesse	98		Dorothy	17
John	98		George	99,100
Margaret	98		Jane	99,100
Mary	98		Joseph	19,99,100
Micael	98		Joyce	100
Robert	19,98,99		Mary	100
Sarah	98,99		Mildred	100
Susanna	98		Ralph	19,100
Thomas	19,98		Richard	100
William	19,98,99		Sarah	3
Sampson, (See Samson)			Susanna	100
Elizabeth	99			
James	99		Shurles,	
John	19,99		Mary	100
Joyce	99,120		Relph	100
Nancy	99		Robert	100
Stephen	99			
Thomas	19,99,120		Simmons,	
Samson, (See Sampson)			Ann	100
Mary	120		Anthony	100
Sanders,			Betsy	100
John	99		Joanna	100
Rebecca	99		Mary	100
			William	100
Sandy,				
Elizabeth	99		Singleton,	
William	99		Ann	100
			Anthony	19,100,120
Saunders,			Averilla	100
Ann	99		Henry	19,100
John	19,99		Isaac	100
Mildred	19		Jean	100
Thomas	19,99		John	100
			Lettitia	100
Sculley,			Lucretia	10
Mary	15		Mary	5
			Pemmy	22,100
Sellers,			Richard	100
Ann	99		William	100
Betty	99		————	100
Mary	99			
Sarah	99		Skelton,	
Thomas	19,99		Elizabeth	6
William	99			
			Smith,	
Shackelford,			Ann	19,101,120
Benjamin	19,99		Armistead	101

Smith, Cont'd
- Baldwin — 101
- Bathsheba — 101
- Betty — 101
- Dorothy — 101,102
- Elizabeth — 4,12,101
- Isaac — 101
- James — 20,101
- John — 101
- Judith — 101
- Margaret Briscoe — 101
- Mary — 101
- Perrin — 101,120
- Peter — 20,101
- Sally — 101
- Sarah — 101
- Susannah — 101
- Thomas — 101,102
- Thomas (Capt.) — 20
- Thomas Buckner — 101
- William — 20,101
- ——— — 102

Smithee,
- Sarah — 11

Snow,
- Cutbud — 102
- Cuthbert — 102
- Cuthbud — 102
- Cuttred — 102
- Jane — 102
- John — 102
- Judith — 102
- Sarah — 102
- William — 102

Soaper, (See Soper)
- Abigail — 3
- Betty — 4
- James — 102
- John — 102
- Joyce — 102

Soles,
- Elizabeth — 11,102
- Mary — 102

Soper, (See Soaper)
- Ann — 102
- James — 120
- John — 20,102
- Joyce — 102
- Mary — 102

Soper, Cont'd
- Mildred — 102
- Priscilla — 102
- William — 102

Spencer,
- Ann — 102
- Elliot — 102
- Mary — 102
- Robert — 20,102
- Sally — 102
- Sarah — 120
- Thomas Hayes — 102

Sprat,
- James — 20,102
- Sarah — 102
- William — 102

Stedar, (See Stedder)
- Ann — 102
- Elizabeth — 102
- John — 102
- Letitia — 102
- Susannah — 102
- Thomas — 102

Stedder, (Stedar)
- Ann — 103
- Betsy — 103
- Dorothy — 18
- Elizabeth — 103
- James — 103
- John — 20,103
- Susanna — 103
- Thomas — 20,103

Stevens,
- Absalom — 103
- Benjamin — 103
- Elizabeth — 103
- Frederick John (Frood) — 120
- John — 103
- Lucy — 103
- Nathaniel — 103
- Robert — 103
- Sarah — 103,121
- Tabitha — 103
- William — 103

Steward, (See Stewart, Stuart)
- Elizabeth — 2
- James — 20
- Joice — 11
- Judith — 21
- ———es — 20

Stewart, (See Steward, Stuart)
 James 103
 John 20,103
 Lettitia 103
 William 103

Stuart, (See Stewart, Steward)
 Armistead 103
 Betsy 103
 Elizabeth Ryland 103
 James 103
 John 103
 Letitia 103
 Margaret 103
 Mary 103
 William 103

Stubberfield,
 Thomas 20

Summers,
 Betty 104
 Jane 65
 John 20,104
 Lucy 121
 Mary 4,104
 Richard 20,104
 Sarah 4
 William 104

T

Tabb,
 Bailey Seaton 104
 Dorothy 7
 Elizabeth 104
 Frances 8,104
 Humphry Foye 20
 John 20,104
 Lucy 5
 Mariana 104
 Martha 15
 Mary 1,4,15,104
 Robert 104
 Susanna 104
 William 104

Tabor,
 Hannah 21
 Joseph 20,104
 Judith 104
 Mary 104

Taylor,
 John 20

Terrell, (See Tyrrel)
 Margaret 104
 Michael 104
 Susannah 104

Terrier,
 Benjamin 104
 Dilly 104
 Eleanor 104
 Elizabeth 11
 John 104
 Mary 15,104
 Philip 20,104
 Thomas 104

Thomas,
 Abraham 104
 Armistead 105
 Ann 15,104,105,106
 Ann Lewis 105
 Anna 14
 Anthony 104
 Elizabeth 5,15,104,105,106
 George 21,105
 George Armistead 105
 Humphry 105,121
 James 21,104,105,106
 James Davis 105
 Jesse 105
 Joel 105
 Johanna 3,106
 John Davis 105
 Josiah 105
 Judith 104,105,106
 Leah 105,106
 Lewis 105
 Mark 21,105,106
 Mary 105
 Matthew 105,106
 Mildred 106
 Morgan 21,105,106
 Rosyann 106
 Sally 106
 Sarah 104,105,106
 Susanna Frances 106
 William 21,104,105,106
 William Bartlet Foster 106
 William Boram 106
 William Edward 106
   9,106

Thornton,
 Sterling 21

Throgmorton,			Treakle, (See Treacle)	
Mordecai	21		Elizabeth	107
Todd,			William	107
Mary	121		Trikle,	
Tomkins, (See Tompkins)			Ann	19
Hannah	106		Turner,	
John	106		Ann	107,108
Mary	4,21		Cynthia Ann	107
Samuel	21		Daniel	107
			Elizabeth	107,108
Tomlin,			George	21,107,108
Ann	106		Hester	107
Elizabeth	106		John	21,107,108
John	106		Joyce	107
Mary	106		Mary	12,107
Samuel	106		Ralph	107
Solomon	106		William	107,108
Tomlinson,			Tyrrel, (See Terrell)	
Elizabeth	11		James	108
			Mary	108
Tomolin,			Michael	21,108
Abigail	22		Nicholas	108
			Susanna	108

W

Tompkins, (See Tomkins)				
Ann	106			
Elizabeth Kemp	106		Wake,	
Elizabeth Simpton	106		Ann	17
John	21			
Mary	17		Walden,	
Mildred	106		Charles	108
Peter	121		James	108
Robert	106		Mary	108
Sarah	18			
William	106		Walker,	
			George	108
Toye,			Mary	108
Elizabeth	22		Matilda	108
Humphry Frances	22,113		Polley Thurston	108
			Robert Dixon	108
Toyes,			Thomas	21
Ann Williams	107			
Henry	107		Waller,	
John	107		Dorothy	108
			Franky	108
Treacle, (See Treakle)			Nelson	108
Dawson	107			
Elizabeth	107		Ward,	
John	21,107		Ann Ross	108
Mary	1,107		Clare	108
Susanna	14,107		Richard Laughlin	108
William	21,107		Thomas	21,108

Washington,			Weymouth,	
Thacker (Gent.)	21		John Davis	109
			Mary	109
Waters,				
Elizabeth	108		White,	
Francis	21,108		Absalom	109,110,111,112
Mary	108		Ann	8,109,112
			Ann Davis	109
Watson,			Ann Elizabeth	109
Hannah	108		Anna	19,109,112
John	21,108		Annah	111,112
Lydia	108		Arthur Bennet	110
Machen Jervis	108		Bartlet	110,112
Mary	108		Cary Washington	110
			Cyrina Wesley	110
Weat,			Cyrus Cary	110
Peter	21		Cyrus James	110
			Dorothy	109,110,111,112
Wedmore,			Dudley	110
Edmond	108		Edward	22,110,111,112
John	108		Edward Chisley	110,121
Sarah	108		Elizabeth	109,110,111 112,113
Welch,			Elizabeth James	110
James Anderton	108		Elizabeth Lee	110
Margaret	20,108		Emery Ann Eliza	110
			Frances	109,110,111,112
Weskom,			George	110
Elizabeth	12		George Washington	110
			Harriet Frances	111
West,			Henrietta Frances	111,121
Benjamin	21		Henry	111
			Hilligan Diggs	111
Westcomb,			Isaac	111
Mary	10		James	22,109,111,112,121
			James Cary	111
Weston,			Jesse	111
Bathsheba	7		John	22,109,110,111,112,113
Betsey	108		John A.	110
Degge	109		John Callis	111
Dolly	109		Joseph	110,111,121
Elizabeth	11		Joseph Davis	111
Frances	108,109		Joyce	4,110,111
Franky	109		Martha W.	110
George	109		Mary	8,22,110,111,112,113
Jenny Stuart	109		Miriam	110,111,121
John	21,109		Nancy	111,112
Judith	109		Nanny	112
Lettitia	109		Paulina	110,112
Major	21,108,109		Pembroke	110,111,112
Mary	8,109		Richard	22,110,111,112
Nanny	109		Robert	112
Robert	109,121		Robert Throckmorton	112
Salley	109		Rosey	112
William	109		Salley	112

(33)

White, Cont'd
    Sarah   6,22,112
    Samuel   112
    Thomas   110,112
    Thomas Bartlet   112
    Thomas Degge James   112
    Wesley Franklin   112
    William   22,109,110
                          111,112,113
    William Henry   112
    William Kitson   112
    ————   113

Whiting,
    Ann   18
    Elizabeth Beverley   2
    Harry Ann   18
    Harriet   113
    Henry   22,113
    Humphry Frances   113
    Judith   113
    Matthew   22,113

Wiatt,
    Benjamin   113
    Margaret   113
    ————   113

Wiley,
    Elizabeth Edwards   113
    Sarah   113
    William   113

Wilkins,
    William   22

Williams,
    Abraham Iveson   113
    Abbigail   113
    Ann   16
    Caty   14
    Daniel   22,113,121
    Elizabeth   2,19,113
    Frances   113,121
    Francis   22,113
    George   113
    Joanna   113,121
    John   22,113,114
    Margaret   113
    Martha   20,113,114
    Mary   10,17
    Nancy Ballard   113
    Patty   113
    Peggy   113

Williams, Cont'd
    Rice   113
    Samuel   113
    Sarah   3,113,114
    Thomas   113,114
    William   22,113,114
    ————   114

Willis,
    Ann   6,114,115,121
    Augustine   114
    Elizabeth   3,17,18,114
    George   114
    Hannah   114
    Henry   22,114
    James   22,114
    Jane   114
    John   22,114,115
    Mary   114,115
    Mildred   114
    Molly   114
    Nancy   114
    Patty   114
    Richard   114
    Salley   114
    Sarah   10,20,114
    Thomas   22,115
    William   22,114,115
    ————   115

Wilson,
    Ann   19
    Caty   115
    James   115
    John   23,115

Wil____
    William   23

Winder, (See Windor, Window
    Ann   15
    Elisabeth   115
    Mary   115
    Thomas   115

Windor,(Winder, Window)
    Thomas   23

Window, (Winder, Windor)
    Ann   115
    Edmond   115
    Elizabeth   115
    James   115
    John   115

Window, Cont'd
    Mary   1
    Molley   115
    Thomas   115

Wise,
    Abel   23

Wi_____,
    Thomas   23

Wooden,
    George   23
    Sarah   121

Wren,
    Elizabeth   115
    John   115
    Kilbe   23,115

Wright,
    Mary   115
    Priscilla   115
    Susannah   115
    William   23,115

Y

Younger,
    Ann   22

CPSIA information can be obtained at www.ICGtesting.com
Printed in the USA
BVOW02s0101140115
383186BV00009B/66/P